TUNNICLIFFE'S COUNTRYSIDE

FROM THE NORTH CAME THE INVADERS, NECKS OUTSTRETCHED,
HUGE WINGS OFFENSIVELY MAGNIFICENT

TUNNICLIFFE'S COUNTRYSIDE

IAN NIALL

CLIVE HOLLOWAY BOOKS

LONDON

First published in Great Britain in 1983 by
Clive Holloway Books
205 Victoria Rise
London SW4 9LJ

General text © Copyright 1983 by Ian Niall

British Library Cataloguing in Publication data
Niall, Ian
    Tunnicliffe's countryside
    1. Tunnicliffe, C. F.   2. Illustrators—England
    I. Title.
    741'.092'4   NC978.5.T/

ISBN 0-907745-02-4

Designed by David Fordham

Filmset by SX Composing Limited, Rayleigh, Essex.
Printed and bound in Great Britain by W. S. Cowell Limited, Ipswich.

CONTENTS

CONTENTS

For Desmond and Jane Reeves

FOTHERINGHAY, A SUPERB CHURCH STANDING LIKE A SMALL LOST
CATHEDRAL OVER THE GRAVES OF KINGS

A DEMONSTRABLY GIFTED MAN

It is quite possible that C. F. Tunnicliffe, had he been born in the city, or had first seen the light of day in a slumland background, might have produced dramatic architectural paintings or peopled his pictures with the kind of characters Lowry loved, but Tunnicliffe's world was a rural one in which the farmyard fowl went to roost in the apple tree and his mother sat in to milk a cow, the way country women had done since time immemorial.

We are, some people insist, products of our environment. Not every country boy chooses to remain there, and few ever aspire to art as did young Tunnicliffe. He was quite small when he first began to draw. Most children take a delight in scribbling on anything to hand but young Charlie's drawings on the whitewash of the shippon and the exterior of his father's new shed were, to say the least, above average. He couldn't be discouraged, and as soon as he was given something more sensible he began to draw the countryside about him; delighting in the content of the landscape, buildings and churches, and the village in which he went to school. These subjects were never to be erased from his recollections of childhood and were the inspiration in a career entirely devoted to art. Even in later years, when he had achieved fame as a bird portraitist, he was continually returning to the farm scene – as he worked on the great many country books that he was commissioned to illustrate.

When a man is successful in what he attempts and people pay tribute, all kinds of tales will be told about how he was discovered and promoted. It wasn't Sir Alfred Munnings, the President of the Royal Academy, who discovered Tunnicliffe as much as Tunnicliffe, the young countryman, who discovered the Academy. Long before this (for his association with the Academy didn't come about for more than twenty years after he had left London and his training at the Royal College) publishers had taken note of the genius evident in his first illustrative commission, Henry Williamson's *Tarka the Otter*.

Again, it wasn't Williamson or his publisher who found Tunnicliffe, for Tunnicliffe, urged to do so by his wife, went out to the River Dane and made drawings which he felt would recommend him to Putnams as the illustrator for Williamson's book, hitherto widely acclaimed as a natural history classic but without illustrations. The flower that wastes its sweetness on the desert air wilts and dies, and similarly the first priority for an artist must be his personal survival, especially in a depression, when young people coming from school or college are finding it difficult to earn their living. There was for this particular young graduate of the Royal College of Art an added incentive and impetus – he was looking after his widowed mother as best he could, and planning to marry.

What Tunnicliffe had in addition to his natural gift was great self-discipline. This discipline sprang from the implanted feeling that if the day's tasks were neglected tomorrow would bring disaster. He had been taught this in the hayfield and the dairy. He had never been lazy, even if country people

INTRODUCTION

BULLOCKS GRAZING ON MIDLAND PASTURES

tended to look upon art as an indulgence, and artists as indolent fellows, dallying with a pencil or a paint-brush on a good hay-making day!

Tunnicliffe drew and painted the things he knew. He offered his pictures to those he thought might appreciate his portraits of birds and animals of the field, and he accepted illustrative commissions for the country books that he had enjoyed reading.

This book covers the years between 1932 and 1977 when he illustrated so many country books that in his old age he could never be sure just how many he had done. In fact there were eighty-eight. He didn't accept every commission offered, but undertook only those books he felt he understood. The biographical observations in his own written masterpieces, *My Country Book, Mereside Chronicle* and *Shorelands Summer Diary* are an endorsement, if any were needed, of his qualifications as an illustrator of the work of other writers.

For many, black-and-white wood-engravings and scraperboards represent the best of Tunnicliffe's work. Their preference has been especially well catered for in the present collection – because, of course, black-and-white accounted for the greater part of the artist's output as an illustrator.

In later life he explained that he wasn't ever "in danger" of being a landscape artist. There were too many landscape artists. His interest had always been in what he called the content of the landscape. Tunnicliffe could, as will be seen in the following pages, decorate an author's work, but he preferred to interpret it. His illustrative contributions not only made the work of Alison Uttley even more attractive to children, but they always educated. Some of his immaculate little drawings are scraper-boards of small creatures, insects, butterflies, bees, newts, frogs or a small bird, quite carried away as it sings to the morning sun and enjoys the sweetness of the summer breeze. Tunnicliffe's wife, Winifred, whose botanical knowledge exceeded his own, was his long stop when it came to vetting his work before submitting it to the publisher. She was determined throughout their life together to see that his immaculate reputation was never going to be tarnished and it never was. It was her less pleasant task to turn away callers so that her husband could get on with what he had to do. Few of those callers had any idea of the physical and mental effort involved in sitting at an easel for ten or more hours a day, day after day, and of his need to get off his treadmill not to talk, but to unwind in peace and rest his tired eyes. Over the years, apart from all the rest of the work he had undertaken to do (supplying commissions for watercolours, and meeting the demands of advertisers who wanted his work to sell their particular products) the most arduous of his labours was to supply the publishers with what they needed for their books. When his initial stint for Henry Williamson was over there was a temporary lull in this work, but just before he was admitted to the Academy his career as a book illustrator took off. The work of H. E. Bates, Negley Farson, Richard Church and even Ernest Hemingway streamed in to

A DEMONSTRABLY GIFTED MAN

HIGH TIDE OVER THE GARDEN WALL

BRIDGE, ROAD, FIELD POOLS AND COB LAKE

THE S-BEND

THE THATCHER,
WITH HIS TARRED TWINE AND PEGS

THE FARMER
VISITING THE VILLAGE SADDLERS

SNOW-CLOGGED HOOVES

A DEMONSTRABLY GIFTED MAN

GULLS FOLLOWING THE PLOUGH

take its place with many others. He met the demand and illustrated *O More Than Happy Countryman, Going Fishing, Green Tide* and *The Old Man and the Sea*. His early work had been almost entirely wood-engraving but this had so taxed his eyesight that he was forced to abandon this more exacting process for scraperboard. In illustration time marches on as it does in everything else. Dürer had had his day, and the great Bewick his when he used the end-grain of the wood for his engraving. Tunnicliffe blamed Williamson, and all the engraving his author had demanded, for his failing eyesight in later life. Whether this was true or not doesn't matter. As a man grows older he learns to compromise and Tunnicliffe certainly went on doing scraperboard illustration to within a couple of years of his death. In scraperboard work an error can be remedied quickly with China white or Indian ink.

If Tunnicliffe regretted his lengthy sessions for Williamson and held them responsible for the trouble with his eyesight when he was in his late seventies, he conveniently forgot, or overlooked the fact that it was twelve years after he had worked on *Tarka* and other Williamson books, that he chose to do his largest wood-engraving. It was one of a heavy horse that brought him recognition from the Academy, to which he was admitted, not as a painter, but as an engraver. Wood-engravings were provided for another and more important country writer in Richard Jefferies' *Wild Life in a Southern County*. Richard Jefferies was the author of at least a dozen classics of natural history, and seeing the work Tunnicliffe did for *Wild Life in a Southern County* one cannot help but wish that he had been commissioned to do other books such as *The Amateur Poacher, Hodge and his Masters, Toilers of the Field* and *The Gamekeeper at Home*. Writers like Bates, Church, Negley Farson and Brian Vesey-Fitzgerald were full of praise for what Tunnicliffe did for them. Alison Uttley, who lived on the other side of the hills that divide Cheshire from Derbyshire but never met him, would have no other artist. My own testament to Tunnicliffe may carry less weight for he was a friend and I was involved with him when he went through a most critical period at the end of his life. We had corresponded but hadn't met when he illustrated the first book, *The Way of a Countryman*. When, in due course, he was asked to do *A Galloway Childhood* he didn't need to go north for he had already been to Galloway and had made sketches. He asked me for a couple of photographs that might give him a certain family background of the period I had written about. When I saw his finished work I was moved by it. He had not only struck a nostalgic chord. He had seen into my mind. The truth was, his countryside and mine had almost everything in common, the old-fashioned ways of husbandry and cultivation, ploughing, sowing, reaping, mowing. We met, and this was confirmed. He undertook to do another book, *To Speed the Plough*, towards the very end of his career. It too, despite his growing disability, had the hallmark of a master, and I shall never forget the enthusiasm he displayed when I telephoned to ask him to undertake this commission.

CANADA GEESE ON THE SHORE OF THE MERE

CHAPTER ONE

A WHIFF OF NOSTALGIA

Extracts from

My Country Book

There was an almost total lack of sentimentality in Charles Tunnicliffe. His feet were firmly on the ground for he had no time for romantic haze. He painted in watercolour, but he was not a Turner fan and Constable landscapes were not for him, though a lot of his work had an air of yesterday about it. He drew his mother or his sister in the long ago days when they worked about that small farm at Sutton Lane Ends by the wind-wafted light of the storm lantern, and came through the mud to the animal warmth of the shippon in which they milked. Nostalgia is invariably the warm recollection of people and places, scents and sounds associated with happiness. No one had been happier than young Tunnicliffe when he was allowed to "idle about with that pencil" and make sketches; when he was Charlie, the boy who hurried from school to get on a pony and go up to the moss and watch a goldfinch, or out to the boundary fence to study a neighbour's earth-pawing bull. Years afterwards he would write about that world in *My Country Book* and embellish what was, without doubt, one of the best books he did with pencil and pastel drawings, scraperboard and watercolours. Some of it was the work of a boy who had yet to graduate from Macclesfield School of Art and go to the Royal College. Consider the quality of that early work, those sketches of the "Fowls in a Damson Tree" and the "Interior of the Shippon"; the pastel drawing, "Milking" and the watercolour, "The Village and Farm from Judy's Lane". These, the "Bull in a Rage" and the "Slumbering Pigs" say something about Tunnicliffe and his inner happiness and explain why he went back to his native place infrequently and reluctantly. He wanted to preserve those cherished images of "The Church and Old Hall Pool" at Gawsworth, "The Plain from the Lee Hills" and the "Stream on Goldsich". He didn't want to revise his mental pictures of Sutton Lane Ends for he knew that time changes everything and invariably destroys the dream when houses crowd into the lanes, when roads are straightened, and bridges over streams are changed from local stone to structures of precast concrete. "I don't want to go back," Tunnicliffe would say almost vehemently. "I don't want to see the place again!" This is his old age, of course, when he was depressed by the thought of radical change. It wasn't that he would have found less in common with the people he might have met again but that they too would have changed. *My Country Book* was enriched with the memories of his boyhood.

LEE FARM

*U*ntil I was nineteen years old I knew little of any other country than my own corner of east Cheshire. Farmwork was never-ending and prevented any holidays but those of a few hours duration. On Sunday mornings, when farm work finished early, it was my habit to climb the hills and to look upon this little domain of mine.

CHARLES TUNNICLIFFE

THE PLAIN FROM THE LEE HILLS

THE VILLAGE AND FARM FROM JUDY'S LANE

*W*alls of dark, rough-hewn stone divided the fields which, in spring and summer, were favourite meeting grounds for lapwings and skylarks, and feeding places for the curlews which nested on the high moors beyond. But the view! Oh, the view was fine! Immediately below me stood Lee Farm (of happy memory; for were we not, as choirboy carollers, taken into the big kitchen and fed on huge potato-pies?) Its fields sloped down to the flat where they joined our own fields. The long low, white house, which was my home, was almost hidden by trees, and glimpses only of it could be seen. Behind it clustered the houses of the village, and, standing apart, the church of St. James could be seen plainly on its own little tombstone-covered hillock.

The prospect westwards was immense, for in that direction the Cheshire Plain stretched away for fifty miles until it was stopped by the first hill outposts of Wales. Many are the mournful occasions on which I have tried to draw the immense landscape as seen from these hills, and often have I been fortified by mugs of tea, which the kindly Ethel of Lee Farm has brought me at my labours. I think the farm folks were a little sorry for me; "Charlie 'ud be better attendin' to th' farm; a dunna think ee'll mak much o' this artist business," seemed to be the general opinion.

CHARLES TUNNICLIFFE

REDESMERE IN SUMMER

Within a radius of three or four miles round the farm I had an intimate knowledge of nearly every yard of ground, and with it I was well content, for it was a full and beautiful countryside. I had the choice of the flat and well-wooded lowlands or the wild heathery moors, as both types of country lay close at hand. There were delightful streams and several sheets of water, some of the latter being man-made, but to me nonetheless attractive for that.

As would be expected, a countryside of such variety supported a correspondingly varied wild animal and bird population, and had I been absolutely unobservant I could not have ignored the hares, rabbits, stoats, weasels, squirrels and hedgehogs, not to mention rats and mice, some of which were seen every day. But I think the birds fascinated me most. From the time the curlews and peewits nested, to the coming of the fieldfares and redwings in the autumn, they were always interesting. Partridges called from the meadows, and on wet autumn days these same meadows would be black with rooks and starlings.

But climb our hills again and see what has happened. Note the nasty pink patches which radiate from the smoky haze which hangs over the heart of Silk-town.

Never again will the peewit nest where these pink blots are. No coveys of partridge will call from them, and no sweet-smelling hay will be gathered there again. When will men realize that green fields are among our most priceless and necessary possessions?

CHARLES TUNNICLIFFE

MOWING, EARLY MORNING

It is four o'clock on a late June morning. The birds are just beginning to tune up, and a slight mist is over everything as I go down the dew-covered pasture to find and catch the black mare. She is inclined to be skittish at first, but soon finds the handful of maize irresistible and comes to my hand without further capers. We go to the stable to harness up, and then down to the meadow to finish a "set" (a section of meadow still to be cut). The mowing machine has been left in the meadow. The mare is backed into the shafts, and soon she is ready for work. The pile of grass which had been put over the cutter-bar of the machine is cleared away, and a newly sharpened knife is pushed into it, and the connecting rod slipped home. Then I get on to the seat and, when the machine is in position for the cutting of the first swathe, the cutter-bar is dropped and with a "suss-a-russ" the grass falls to the flashing knife and is turned by the arm of the grass-board into even swathes. Down they go, grasses, daisies, sorrels, and a few thistles (curse them, for they prick when loading hay with bare arms). The mare is inclined to take things with a rush at first, but soon settles down to a steady pace, and sweat begins to show at the edge of her collar and saddle.

By six o'clock the sun is beginning to dispel the mists and up at the farm the cows are just going into the shippons for the morning's milking. Round and round the set goes the mowing machine. The grass which was first cut is losing its fresh green and is already taking on a blue tinge. Gradually the set diminishes in area, and eventually one end of it becomes a point, as the set was not a perfect rectangle in the first place. Now it is quickly reduced in size, and by ten o'clock I am cutting the last thin line of standing grass.

CHARLES TUNNICLIFFE

INTERIOR OF THE SHIPPON

Patterns of hoar frost curl over the diamond panes of the bedroom window through which the light of the setting moon gleams dully. I watch the light from the warmth of my bed for a time, putting off the evil moment of getting up for as long as possible. Father and mother are already astir; I hear the clatter of milk-cans below, and cannot safely delay any longer. How cold and clammy these cord trousers are this frosty morning!

The lantern light strikes white sparks from the hoar frost, and gleams on the yard-long icicles which hang from the eaves and spoutings of the buildings. The yard is iron-hard and, in the frosty air, my breath is visible as a grey cloud.

How welcome is the warmth which greets me as I open the shippon door! Some of the cows are already standing up; others, with lazy grunts, get up as I enter. Buckets of corn are dumped at the heads of the first three cows to be milked, and soon father, mother, and myself are making the pails ring with the first streams of milk.

CHARLES TUNNICLIFFE

MILKING

THE CHURCH AND OLD HALL POOL, GAWSWORTH

Gawsworth has ever been a favourite haunt of mine. There is an air about the place which attracts me, whatever the time of the year. It is quiet and detached, away from the busy traffic of the main road, yet it never appears sleepy. The Elizabethan age seems to have impressed its lively and stimulating mark upon the place, and I will never pooh-pooh the story that the ghost of Mary Fytton (that Mary who is supposed to have been Shakespeare's "Dark Lady") is seen occasionally in the church. Indeed, I should not be in the least surprised to see Queen Elizabeth and a crowd of courtiers on the lawn of the Old Hall, or moving in stately procession to the tilting ground beyond.

CHARLES TUNNICLIFFE

STARTLED HERON

BIRDS OF THE NEW HALL

The pool would reflect perfectly the image of the black-and-white Old Hall were it not for a party of mad mallard which dash over, and sometimes underneath, its surface. Three drakes are chasing one duck. She takes flight, the drakes following her, and alights among the daffodils and bushes of flowering currant by the Old Hall lawn. As the drakes alight by her side she takes to wing again; and so the mad courtship goes on, the drakes capering and posturing on the water, and giving the poor duck no peace. . . .

The mallard here have attracted many wild birds of their kind. There is a pair of tame Barnacle Geese, which this fine morning seem to be unusually excited, for they dash spasmodically about the lawn as if to take wing. But one wing of each bird is pinioned, and this causes them to run in a curve. Perhaps their instinct tells them that it is high time they were away to the Northern nesting grounds of their species.

CHARLES TUNNICLIFFE

CANADA GEESE RISING

SLUMBERING PIGS

*P*igs *are very good to draw. They have interesting form and, providing they are not too fat, are quite beautiful. But they should be approached carefully, for if they are surprised they do not settle again easily. Often have I crept cautiously to the door of the sty and, on seeing the pigs asleep, have started to draw them. Then, perhaps, I have made a slight noise. One pig immediately opens its pale blue eyes and, on seeing my head above the door, gives a startled bark and jumps up; the others, without waiting to find the cause of the disturbance, do likewise and rush away, probably into the darkest recesses of the sty. Make no mistake, pigs are most intelligent animals!*

But perhaps the best way to know the true shape of any animal is to handle it, and there were certain days in winter when the handling of pigs was unavoidable; days when the butcher would come, with his bag of knives and rope nooses, and slaughter the fat ones. How they would struggle!

Handling the pig afforded ample opportunity to become familiar with the shape of legs, shoulders and haunches.

CHARLES TUNNICLIFFE

FOWLS ROOSTING IN A DAMSON TREE

In the summer evenings the young poultry go to roost on places other than the perches provided for them. They will settle on the chicken coop, on the shafts of the tipped-up carts, and in any convenient bush or tree. On tree branches they usually arrange themselves in beautiful groups. One evening in spring I saw an exquisite sight. A white Leghorn cock and four hens had gone to roost in a damson tree which was in full bloom. The combination of white, brown and chequered fowl and starry white bloom on thin black twigs, backed by a delicate spring evening sky, was a joy to behold.

CHARLES TUNNICLIFFE

THE GANDER

CROAKING CUCKOO

In many of my bird paintings I have found that the area of my picture covers only about a square yard of ground and, as this is always a very vital part of the design, I have found it necessary to make careful detail studies of the typical surroundings of the birds. Some time ago I painted a party of teal in early spring. The studies of the teal were made from a group of wild birds feeding in a pool in a swamp. Their surroundings consisted of clumps of dead reed-grass, dull ochreous-cream in colour, the bright cloud-reflecting water, and a lovely detail which fixed the time of the year – namely the fresh green spears of young reed-grass. It seemed exactly the right setting for the teal, and I made very careful notes of both the dead grass and the new shoots. The pattern made by nature was far more wonderful than anything that I could have invented. Indeed, nature is the master pattern maker.

CHARLES TUNNICLIFFE

TEAL AMONG THE REED-GRASS

BULL IN A RAGE

When I was a boy, one of my favourite pastimes was to imitate the low bellowing of a bull, and then to watch the effect on one in the next field. Up would go his head, as he gave an answering bellow, and soon he would be clearing all the cows of his herd away from the vicinity of the fence, behind which I was concealed. Then, uttering low, throaty growling, he would advance, intermittently stopping to paw the ground with his fore-feet, and sending turf and sods flying into the air. With bloodshot eyes, saliva-dripping mouth, and nose close to the ground, he would look an awesome sight. Arriving at the fence, and not sighting his antagonist, he would indulge in a goring orgy, tearing at the roots of the hawthorns with his horns and feet, and making the most horrible noises. No other bull appearing, he would gradually quieten down and shamble off to his herd, with his horns encrusted with soil from the hedge back, and perhaps a foxglove stalk dangling from his head.

CHARLES TUNNICLIFFE

THE SHIRE STALLION

*T*he magnificent shire stallion is a very early memory. As far back as I can remember I seem to have been thrilled by these grand creatures. Whenever one went striding past the farm gate, bedecked with ribbons and plaits, I would follow it as far as possible, and try to beg a card from its attendant groom. This card usually bore a photograph of the stallion and its pedigree and points. As boys we used to discuss stallions and their qualities as boys today discuss aeroplanes.

Twice a year a parade of stallions was held in Silk-town. From all over east and mid-Cheshire they were brought to this parade, there to show off their paces and points to the crowds of farmers and horsey folk gathered for the occasion. A crowd of farmers would gather round each horse and there was much feeling of the stallions' leg bones, examination of hooves, and discussions with the grooms on the horses' particular qualities. Cards of pedigree were handed round, but never to boys who coveted them.

CHARLES TUNNICLIFFE

STAGS-HEAD WEIR, RIVER BRAY

Henry Williamson was busy on another book, this time about the life cycle of an Atlantic salmon, and, acting upon his warning that illustrations would be needed, I took every opportunity to study salmon and their ways. My search took me into Wales, Scotland, Lancashire and Devon.

One day in October I received a telegram from Devon which read "RIVER IN SPATE SALMON RUNNING." The evening of that day found me on a train heading for the West Country, and next morning I was in the heart of Devon. Much rain had fallen and low heavy clouds still blotted out the tops of the hills. Everywhere was soaking, and, as I made my way from the little station to the thatched cottage in the valley, water gushed along every roadside channel, taking with it the brown October leaves.

After a hurried breakfast and some precise directions from my host I made my way to the river. It was running swift and strong down the valley, the water a leaden-green in colour, and bank-high. Presently, above the noise of the swift water, a dull rumbling could be heard which, as I continued down river, grew louder and louder. Over the weir near the sawmill the grey-green river rushed, and the thunder of its fall filled the place with a pulsating roar which drowned every other sound. At the foot of the fall was a tumult of white water on which I fixed my attention. For a few minutes nothing happened; then, suddenly, out of the boil leapt a dark, thirty-inch-long fish. It leapt high and true in a graceful arc with all its paired fins pointing downwards, but the weir was high, and the female salmon landed with a splash on a shelf in the weir, where, for several seconds, she quivered and beat her tail, and then fell back.

CHARLES TUNNICLIFFE

RED-THROATED DIVERS

Travelling about and delving into the mysteries of countrysides other than my own did but whet my appetite for more, and one of my unaccountable desires was to see a landscape of rock, without trees or hedges, or any of the rich growth to which I had been accustomed. So, one memorable September I found myself in Iona, an island of the Inner Hebrides. Here was my rocky landscape, treeless except for a few small sycamores near the village, and an atmosphere that had an exquisite, unearthly quality impossible to describe. Much of my time there, when not occupied in gazing at land and sea, was spent peering through field glasses at birds, many of which visited Iona on their migration flight. Birds among this rocky landscape seemed doubly attractive, everything washed so clean, birds so immaculate, and distances so wonderful that I never wanted to leave.

CHARLES TUNNICLIFFE

A STREAM ON GOLDSICH

SPARROWHAWK

"*T*arka the Otter" was but one of a series of four books which I illustrated for
H. Williamson, and all threw me into closer and closer contact with animals and
birds. One book especially, entitled "The Peregrine's Saga", I consider had a marked
influence on the future trend of my work. While I was making studies of the Peregrine
falcon, my work led me to a meet of the Falconry Club whose members were flying their
hawks at Avebury in Wiltshire. In a paddock, behind the village, I found their hawks
and falcons tethered to perches and blocks on the grass under a line of bosky lime trees. I
shall never forget the thrill I had at the first sight of those birds, all feather-perfect and
fighting fit. There sat the devilishly fierce Goshawks and Sparrowhawks, side by side
with the dark-eyed, haughty Peregrines, while in another enclosure were the dainty
Merlins, the little falcons of my own east Cheshire and Derbyshire moorlands. I
worked by the side of these birds day after day, making copious notes of their poses and
plumage, and several times I went on to the Downs with the falconers to see the
Peregrines trying their young wings against the wily rook.

CHARLES TUNNICLIFFE

HEAD OF A YOUNG TIERCEL

ADULT GOSHAWK

A

t the end of the line was a fine adult goshawk, a bird greater in size and fierceness than any peregrine. It sat upright and still, its cruel yellow feet grasping the leather padding of the bow-perch. But the feet were not so cruel as the yellow-ringed eyes, which glared at every moving thing, and did not miss the smallest bird which passed over. I was fascinated by this hawk and could not resist the chance to draw it. A front view of the bird's head was one of the most devilish things I had ever beheld.

CHARLES TUNNICLIFFE

BLACKFACE RAM AND EWES

CHAPTER TWO

THE FARM SCENE

Extracts from

Both Sides of the Road

n his earliest attempts to sketch with chalk, scribbling on the walls of the shippon when his father put a stop to his use of the boards of his new shed, young Tunnicliffe drew animals. He had an eye for the angles of bones thrusting against the skin of a cow as she made ungainly progress over rough ground. He captured the natural symmetry of fat young pigs slumbering contentedly in the straw of the piggery, as well as the flap-eared, knowing expression of the old sow peering short-sightedly to see if her visitor had brought a pail of mash or simply come to prod her out of her sty so that it could be cleaned. Young Tunnicliffe was also fascinated by large animals, that towering mountain of horseflesh that was a braided stallion held so confidently on a halter by a groom and the quite unstoppable traction of a bull going at a rival with head down and horns weaving lethally. The first birds he drew were chickens. He loved bantams that scratched in the farmyard, dustbathed in dry places and laid away in the deep shadows of a large bush or the secret corners of some outbuilding. These things were his first inspiration, to be exploited to the full when he was a young married man doing art work for advertising firms; but he kept a lot to himself, and the very essence of it all was distilled for *Both Sides of the Road*, a book that proved a most brilliant collaboration between artist and writer, the author in this case being Rogerson. *Both Sides of the Road* was every bit as good as *Shorelands Summer Diary*, although the latter was, of course, a personal testament giving a deeper insight into what made Tunnicliffe tick.

Tunnicliffe told me once that *Both Sides of the Road* was really a bonus for all his sessions doing farm animals for commercial concerns. It came, he said, "like water off a duck's back" even if it wasn't a bird book. In addition to his field sketching he had taken great trouble to make himself familiar with almost every breed of cattle, sheep and pig. He knew his horses, as Sir Alfred Munnings had already discovered. He was to please all his fans and admirers with his farm scenes, and farmers who knew sheep appreciated that here was an artist who knew the Downland breeds, Leicester, Hardwick and Blackface. Those who bred pigs saw that he knew Saddlebacks and Tamworths. When it came to farm machinery (things having changed from that long ago day when he had used the horse reaper to cut hay, breaking a draught pole on at least one occasion) Tunnicliffe went to the implement makers and then out into the fields to see the mechanical monsters at work. Half of what he did stemmed from instinct for what was right. He had fed his pig. He had milked his cow and straddled the pony to ride to the moor. He knew that the farm scene was a hundred miles away from the sentimental dream. It was, like Lorenz's goslings, imprinted in his mind and in his old age he knew exactly how horses stood to a draught pole, how they turned the plough on the headland or backed in under the saddle chain on a cart. It is true to say that *Both Sides of the Road* could hardly be faulted by either an artist or a farmer, but the artist's acknowledged inspiration owed a great deal to his beloved childhood at Sutton Lane Ends.

AN OLD COWSHED

*I*n almost all old farm buildings the animals' quarters are dark and devoid of proper ventilation, and animals can no more thrive without light and fresh air than humans. My olfactory memory at once registers the difference between a modern cow-house, high, light, airy and disinfected daily, and the old mistals or shippons of the Yorkshire Dales. How well I can savour in memory those low-roofed, ill-lit caverns, heavy with a scent compounded of the smell of hay and the sweet breath of the beasts, but so charged with ammonia that it set eyes and nose a-tingle. By contrast, the modern cow-house has, as I have already noted, the clean and sterilised atmosphere of a hospital ward.

The newer type of milk farmers have installed up-to-date plant and equipment, and employ the most modern and hygienic methods of dairying. Yet time and again you will discover that these white-tiled, chromium-plated affairs have been built into the farm to suit architectural convenience and without due regard to the other daily activities. I have in my mind's eye several farms where the cows as they are driven in to milk have to cross the paths of men on other jobs, and even, on one farm, the path to the front of the dwelling-house, so that these are inevitably fouled and churned up in wet weather.

I think that if we are honest we must recognize that one of the important tasks before British farmers is to give their farmsteads the same sort of care that has been for years devoted to the layout of factories or colliery pit-heads.

SIDNEY ROGERSON

MODERN COW-TYING AND DRINKING BOWLS

TURNING THE HAY, OLD STYLE

FELL-SIDE HAY-SLEDGE

*H*aymaking, or haysel, is a joyous time. It cannot be called the crown of the farming year, for that is deservedly the title of harvest-home, but haysel is, to my idea, the most exhilarating of farming occasions. Hay is the first of the farm's crops to be harvested, and over most of England and Wales it is brought home at a season of the year when the promise of spring is still unfulfilled, when "God's in His heaven, all's right with the world". This joyousness is clearly reflected in pictures of haymaking scenes in days long ago. Then haysel was a yearly picnic when every one on the farm, men, women and little children, turned out to make merry, but also to work. Indeed, every available pair of hands, however small, was needed to ensure that the work was done as quickly as possible, and so lessen the ever-present threat of bad weather. Some of the same spirit still characterises haysel today, when the process is almost wholly mechanised, and machines for making, collecting and for baling or stacking the hay have reduced the human labour force to a minimum. Yet the wives and the sweethearts, the sisters and sons are still drawn to the meadows, still feel it necessary to be there at the year's first harvest-home. . . .

Haymaking is one of the oldest practices of the farm, perhaps the original method of conserving food for the winter when animals cannot go out to graze but must be fed in the stalls or yards of the farm buildings. The grass is allowed to grow almost to ripeness, and is then cut with a reaper drawn by a tractor or, especially if the meadow is small, by a horse or horses. The cut grass lies in swathes, and the idea is for sun and wind to dry it so that it will keep dry and sweet throughout the winter and, if necessary, possibly for two *SIDNEY ROGERSON* winters. To speed this drying process the grass is turned either by hand or by a mechanical swathe-turner and then made into heaps, which may be called either haycocks or pikes, according to the part of Britain.

PERCHERONS

A

lthough there are hilly and mountainous districts where farmers and
shepherds ride ponies or cobs in the course of their daily work, the only
class of horse really necessary to modern farming is the heavy draught animal,
of which there are five varieties, three British and two alien. The most popular
and widely distributed of our native horses is the Shire, a name which seems
misleadingly to indicate that the breed was originally developed in the
"Shires", which today are associated rather with the lighter classes of riding
horse, known loosely as hunters. . . .

The Shire has all the qualities required of a heavy draught animal. It is
immensely strong, it is a "good doer" – which is to say it makes the maximum
bone, muscle and energy from the food it is given – and, so long as speed or
sudden haste is not demanded of it, has great powers of endurance. Most
important, it has an equable temperament, always docile and often
phlegmatic. This is essential, for in the course of its daily duties it will
constantly be required to stand still for long spells – while the cart or tumbril it
is drawing is being loaded or off-loaded, say, or while adjustments are being
made to plough or harrow – without becoming restive or impatient, no matter
that it may be pestered by the attentions of flies and mosquitoes or have its
nerves jarred by the sudden, machine-gun rattle of the rival tractor. It would be
hopeless to employ on farm work a horse with the nervous, highly-strung
temperament of the thoroughbred. Equability of temperament is another
characteristic of British farm animals, few of which have to be classed as of
uncertain or unreliable temper.

The English Shire is, in short, the embodiment of "slow but sure", but it
is not at first sight very different from its Scottish cousin, the Clydesdale, and
indeed you may well be forgiven if for a start you confuse the one with the
other. The Clydesdale has much the same build and is used for much the same
purposes. It is big, it is heavy, it has feathered legs and it is of the same bay
colour.

40

SHIRE STALLION

SHEARING, EAST CHESHIRE

CHILLINGHAM CATTLE

CLYDESDALE MARE AND FOAL

TAMWORTH GILTS AND GLOUCESTER OLD SPOTS SOW

CARTING MANGOLDS TO THE CLAMP

he stacks stand out in all winds and weathers, until one day the threshing engine comes, with its brass horse prancing bravely on its plate, its black-faced driver and his load of coal, to complete the cycle of seed-time and harvest by separating the grain from the rustling bones of the plant which bore it. With the engine – and nowadays a small and un-beautiful stationary tractor will often do duty for the noble, black steam engine which looks like the half-sister to a steam roller – will come the lumbering threshing machine; and its attendant elevator. The engine and thresher will be coupled up close to the stacks, whether in the farm's yard or in the corner of a field. Men standing on the stack pass the sheaves with two-tined forks, or pitchforks, to other men who cut the string binding the sheaves and feed them into the machine, the grain running out at the tail of the machine into sacks. At the opposite end, the empty, threshed straw will be made into another stack, so that as the one stack slowly wastes the other rises as the elevator with its endless chain of teeth carries the straw up to men who pitch it into proper shape. For a little while, a few days at most, something of the urgency and bustle of harvest returns. The stackyard is a scene of ordered animation, each man fitting into the picture with the ease of training and experience. Against the sky the pitchers on the stacks work with an unhurried rhythm, which contrasts sharply with the excited movements of those on the ground, the foreman shouting orders, the comings and goings of the men loading and carrying the sacks, the alternate lolling and shovelling of the engine-man and his mate, and ever and anon the flailing rush as the rat-catchers, professional and self-appointed, fall on the rats which bolt squealing from the stacks. All this action goes on to the orchestration of the throb of the engine, the bass hum of the thresher and the rattle and click of the elevator. The air is thick with flying dust-motes and particles of straw, which sparkle as the sunlight picks them out. So twelve months or more from the day it was sown, the wheat, or oats, or barley, at last leaves the farm for the mills, there to be ground into food for the nourishment of Man and Beast.

THRESHING

LARGE WHITE PIGS

LARGE BLACK SOW AND LITTER

The pig is the animal closest to man, lodged often within a few yards of the farmhouse, and frequently fed direct by the housewife with waste from her kitchen. Even when the farmer keeps pigs for profit instead of to fatten for his own bacon, the pens or houses seem automatically to become a place of rendezvous where the farmer and his friends forgather to smoke their pipes and argue over the weights of the inmates. But then the pig is a peculiar person, unlike any of the other farm animals – except the farmer himself. That is not meant as disparagement of the farmer, but merely a way of saying that the pig is the most human of the domestic animals. What I mean is excellently described by an old saying which I have quoted more than once, that "a dog looks up to you, a cat looks down on you, but a pig looks upon you as another human being". If you ever happen to have anything to do with pigs you will soon learn how true this is – how they cannot resist poking their noses, literally and metaphorically, into anything that is going on, yet with what unconcern they carry themselves.

The poor pig has been reviled down the ages as the embodiment of gluttony and sloth. Of course it is greedy, very greedy. It is this natural greed which enables it, if properly fed, in a very short time to make flesh and fat for pork, bacon and lard. But it is Man who has played on this trait, who has carried out selective breeding to develop it and who keeps his pigs in conditions which encourage them to eat to make weight and denies them normal exercise to work it off. That is one reason why you seldom see pigs roaming about the fields or wastelands in search of their own food. To permit them to do so would be to increase the time it takes for them to reach the stage when they will give an efficient return in meat and fat for the food they have been given.

SIDNEY ROGERSON

A WHEEL PLOUGH

For centuries the plough was a simple affair with two handles and one blade or ploughshare to bite into the earth and turn it up: steered by a man and drawn by two horses. Horse-ploughing is a craft, and the experienced ploughman is an expert in managing his horses and in drawing his furrow straight as a ruler. His hands are needed not only to steer the plough, which is a task demanding skill as well as strength, but also to guide the horses by means of cords, or sometimes by one cord only. The truth is that they usually act more on the orders the ploughman sings out to them. . . .

Once the land ploughed in autumn is dry enough, it may be cultivated as well as harrowed and rolled in early spring. The cultivator is a machine which is designed to loosen the under-soil without turning it over; that is, it does its work by means of long, sharp claws which work well beneath the surface to the full depth of the furrow the plough makes, or even below. The idea is to make sure that the soil is aerated and permeable, and not just worked on top and a solid mass underneath.

SIDNEY ROGERSON

CABBAGE FIELD

THINNING OUT THE PLANTS

*T**here remain the less romantic crops of arable farming – roots, kales, cabbages, potatoes, peas and beans, and the varied list of specialist and near-market-garden crops.*

The main root crops are turnips, mangolds, swedes and sugar-beet, though there are, of course, others like red-beet or beetroot, kohl rabi, and parsnips, which scarcely qualify as farm crops proper. They, and indeed all arable crops, are cultivated by the same general methods as grain. The important difference with roots and the kales and cabbages and others is that the gaps between the rows in which they have been drilled will need periodical clearing of weeds, either by hand-hoeing or, more usually, by horse-drawn or mechanical hoer. When the crop begins to come through in crowded rows of tiny plants they will need thinning out or "singling" by hoeing, a gap of about nine inches being left between one plant and the next. This work must be done by hand.

SIDNEY ROGERSON

THE CULTIVATOR

A FLOCK OF WILD DUCK CLATTERED FUSSILY UP FROM THE REEDS

THE FIRST MILESTONE

Extracts from

A Book of Birds; A Fowler's World; A Galloway Childhood; Beasts Royal; Bird Portraiture; Dawn, Dusk and Deer; Exploring England; Going Fishing; Green Tide; In the Heart of the Country; O More Than Happy Countryman; Our Bird Book; Rivermouth; R.S.P.B. Book of Garden Birds; Salar the Salmon; Tarka the Otter; The Leaves Return; The Lone Swallows and Other Tales; The Long Flight; The Old Stag; The Way of a Countryman; Walking with Fancy; Wild Life in a Southern County.

The road to success so far as Tunnicliffe was concerned was the long, winding, country road along which he stopped occasionally to make reference drawings of birds. With animals, and farm animals in particular, there was less need for reference. He knew most of them too well to need any kind of aid to memory. He not only knew the shape of the horse but the very feel of its flank, its neck, its shoulder. He could probably have drawn any of the domestic animals blindfolded. Not every writer has the dual talent of being both articulate, and able to draw what he sees. There have, of course, been some exceptions, and a few upon whom the gods have smiled as they did on Beatrix Potter. Tunnicliffe was not paid vast sums for his illustrating work, but he didn't have a bargain basement. Invariably demand governed the fee for something publishers recognized as almost unequalled knowledge of the country scene.

No one paid him for being born with a gift, although they knew his talent was rare indeed. In Devon he had been harnessed to an arrogant taskmaster, Henry Williamson, who was determined to have things his way regardless of the fact that Tunnicliffe was working for a mere pittance. "Get sketching!" he once yelled at Tunnicliffe on one occasion when hounds were in for the kill, everyone standing by and no one preventing the slaughter. Tunnicliffe, knowing that even his uncanny gift for capturing movement with a pencil and sketchpad was inadequate, used a camera, and further upset Williamson!

No one who has read *Tarka* can have any doubt of Williamson's sensitivity, and if Tunnicliffe was a degree more down-to-earth in his approach one may nevertheless ponder the state of his mind when one looks at those rather sombre woodcuts of hound and huntsman. Did he entirely approve of otter hunting? He is no longer here to tell us, but his work speaks for him.

Tunnicliffe felt himself badly exploited by both his publishers and Williamson. The royalty was Williamson's. The artist's fee on the first occasion was fifty pounds out of which he paid his fare to Devon. Alas, he had agreed and signed before he knew what was involved. He was still reluctant to make a stand over the other books for he was, after all, pulling himself up on Williamson's coat-tails, at least for the time being. *Tarka* was the countryside of Williamson's fantasy but what Tunnicliffe brought to the book was realism. In it were no less than 23 full-page wood-engravings in addition to a frontispiece and 16 line vignettes. Some measure of the task may be appreciated when one learns that *The Lone Swallows*, appearing the following year, 1933, had the same number of wood-engravings and twice the number of vignettes. This was followed by *The Old Stag*, again with 23 wood-engravings and 9 vignettes. That ill-fated novel, *The Star Born*, appeared a month later and it had 15 full-page and 19 vignetted wood-engravings. There was also a wood-engraving specially done for the jacket of this novel which Tunnicliffe swore he didn't understand and illustrated with great reluctance. A year later,

CHAPTER THREE

CHINESE AND CANADA GEESE

in 1934, Putnam published Williamson's *The Peregrine's Saga*. It had a frontispiece and 12 full-page engravings, but Tunnicliffe was perhaps tiring a little and welcomed *Salar the Salmon*, a commission from Faber executed in scraperboard and watercolour, 16 full-page colour plates and some 70 vignetted scraperboards, head and tail pieces. This was the end of the collaboration of Williamson and Tunnicliffe.

There is a saying that as one door closes another opens. Although the record indicates the occasional lull in Tunnicliffe's output as an illustrator, the door was never to close. Good work speaks for itself and he never needed to submit anything to solicit a commission after that offering to Putnam in the early 1930s. The work of many celebrated writers came his way. Not least was that of H. E. Bates in a "seasons of the year" series – *The Seasons and the Gardener* – which may surprise those who have read novels such as the *Purple Plain*. It was probably the popularity of these small books by Bates that encouraged Frank Whittaker of *Country Life* to ask Tunnicliffe to do one called *In the Heart of the Country*. He was also happy to become Whittaker's artist for *Country Life Annual*. The work of Negley Farson, *Going Fishing*, was an angling classic and a highly suitable follow-up for Country Life Books. The association of Bates, Tunnicliffe and Whittaker paved the way for my book *The Way of a Countryman*, published in 1965 by Country Life Books. Publishers took their place in the queue and at times seemed to leapfrog one another as Tunnicliffe sup-

plied work that delighted the critics as well as everyday readers. In his day, Bates wrote to express his approval. He was content to leave things to Tunnicliffe, he said, because Tunnicliffe knew what was needed. Negley Farson wrote to the artist to pay a personal tribute. Brian Vesey-Fitzgerald, a warmhearted man, was equally gracious and said he only wished his work was as good as the artist's. Excerpts from some of the books show how well Tunnicliffe got into the spirit of the work he illustrated. It went on and on like this and (to anyone who might imagine that Tunnicliffe confined himself to birds and those farm animals he did so well for the commercial scene and the world of advertising) it needs to be pointed out that he was equally at home drawing and producing illustrations for books such as Arthur Cadman's *Dawn, Dusk and Deer*. He was the illustrator of that remarkably well done book, Richard Patrick Russ's *Beasts Royal*. It was field study that enabled him to make such a good job of Arthur Cadman's book but whether he waited patiently to see a deer or fawn cross a leafy glade or went to the zoo for his gorilla to complete *Beasts Royal*'s fine list of wash drawings, monochrome, it was plainly a talent for the anatomy of animals that enabled him to do such wonderful work.

Tunnicliffe's many talents have been generally recognized since his death. As a bird artist people tended to look for his work in the galleries and at the Academy, but those who followed his star from the beginning knew the brilliance to be discovered in a multitude of major and minor illustrations to be

ROE BUCK

found in *A Book of Birds* (superb wood-engraving) and *Bird Portraiture,* a veritable artist's handbook on the subject – supposing the student has anything approaching the same gift. At the period when he was teaching art at Manchester Grammar, and suffering the frustrations of trying to teach youngsters taking his subject only in order to fill out a syllabus, Tunnicliffe evidently felt the need to put it all down for the more dedicated. In his book on bird portraiture he was offering inspiration, as he was in the wonderful colour work he produced for the R.S.P.B.'s *Garden Birds* by Linda Bennett and brought out for the Society by Hamlyn.

All through his working life Tunnicliffe never let up or reduced his standard. The long road to success as an illustrator ran beside his triumph as a painter and few, if any illustrator, before or since has done as much or been so admired.

Tunnicliffe's Countryside is more than a mere gleaning of a great harvest of illustration. It is an indication of the breadth of the artist's personal landscape. His father had been a village shoemaker and Tunnicliffe gives us his Village Cobbler. He had lived where the gypsies brought their wagons to rest. He knew the great horses that brought sheaves to the rickyard in *A Galloway Childhood.* He had seen the deer, as Richard Jefferies described them in *Wild Life in a Southern County,* and the expression on the face of the hunting stoat.

He hardly needed to go back to the sea to check his seals, or to the river to look at otter cubs again. Birds flew in his imagination. The geese rose and beat their way over the snowy field and the rook perched on the telegraph pole. Only a great poet could have rivalled this ability to see things, quite so clearly, in the mind.

GREAT CRESTED GREBE

INLAND IS MONOTONY

The Shetlands are a paradox. The very islands themselves do not look like islands but seem an ice-rubbed, battered mountain range that has suddenly sunk below its timber line into the sea. There are over a hundred islands. The biggest, Mainland, which takes up over three-fourths of all the surface, is fifty four miles long by twenty one wide; yet a man can stand in the very middle of it at Mavis Grind and throw a stone into either the North Sea or the Atlantic.

The coastline is crazy. It is a sort of geologic debauch where the rocks seem to have gone mad. They shoot out of the sea in sheer cliffs, spear points and great arches through which one could sail a full-rigged sailing ship. Gulls, guillemots, fulmar petrels, shags, and puffins scream from the serrated edges of the cliffs, shoot past in staring flotillas on the tide, and whirl in feathered spray over the onrushing green waves.

Inland is monotony: black peat bogs and the long, lonely moors: the cry of the curlew. There are no streams, only a few gurgling burns which run almost unseen along the black channels they have dug through the peat to empty into shallow, wind-swept lochs, where the water lies black as coffee before the cream is poured in. Drear country, mostly given over to the grazing of sheep; crofting country, where the farmer-fishermen live in little thatched stone huts by the shore, huts crouching, it seems, with their heads down against the sea wind, their thatch held on by old nets and heavy stones.

NEGLEY FARSON

THIS WAS THE HOME OF THE SEALS

*C*liffs rise above, towering overhead to break off in turreted battlements against the rounded clouds. Black ravens sail out of them, hanging in the vast emptiness. The rocks are red, mauve, scarlet. Walls, leaning towers, two-hundred-foot spear-points of red granite.

    This was the home of the seals. When we weren't fishing we searched for them among these fantastic red rocks.

NEGLEY FARSON

THE SIZE DOES NOT ALWAYS MATTER

*A*s *the afternoon went on and the sun grew warmer and
the voices of the girls drowsier under the warm-scented apple-
trees, and the light more vivid on the white and crimson corn-barn and
the claret lily-leaves, I began to understand something of what fishing
is about – why it has remained so deeply in the affections of men, why
it has never become an expression of collective social snobbery, why it
brings out the best and not the worst of a man's nature.*

H. E. BATES

58

WHERE THE DARK RIVERS CURVE DOWN FROM EXMOOR

The gentle art of stream fishing in the West Country of England has a charm all of its own. Perhaps that is just why I have never tried to fish for salmon on this river, although I have certainly fished it double the number of times I have fished any loch or river in Scotland. As I have said, I enjoy the luxury of my own solitude, my own idle reflections – the inner solitude. There are times when I don't want trouble, I don't want thrills; I have come here for just a lazy contentment.

NEGLEY FARSON

AN IMPERTURBABLE SCENE
WHICH FILLS YOU WITH CONTENTMENT

I think the best thing to call it is a certain quiet decency. This almost unchanging English scene, with its red and green rolling hills, holds a romance that wild rocks, and wild rivers, or snow-capped volcanoes could never give you. It has a gentleness, a rich rustic worth, and an unostentatiousness that is like the English character. An imperturbable scene which fills you with contentment.

Here with a little aluminium box in your pocket, or a few flies stuck in your coat lapel, you will fish all day with a cast so fine that it looks like a strand of a brunette's hair.

NEGLEY FARSON

THE CLOUD GREW

They moved to the boat where it was drawn on the hard, and sitting on the thwarts, contemplated the afternoon. Over the rim of the hills a cloud was building, and to this the gillie's eyes were turned. It was no part of his employment to wish ill to his charges, however they compared with his real master. The laird would wish him to give of his best, and the best he had given, with few words, but with punctuality and courtesy.

The cloud grew. It swelled as though it were being blown up by a bellows, and it mounted the sky.

TERENCE HORSLEY

BROWN TROUT

*T*hese were light-backed trout with vivid red spots, which struck (when they did strike) with a vicious intensity. This river was not a glacial one, and in that ice-clear water I could watch a large part of their fight. In one deep stretch of river, where it was so flat and slow that it was almost like a shallow lake, I got the best fish of the afternoon by putting on an old worn Mayfly. It was a freak attempt, but continuous rises under the branches of some trees on the far side of the pool tempted me.

NEGLEY FARSON

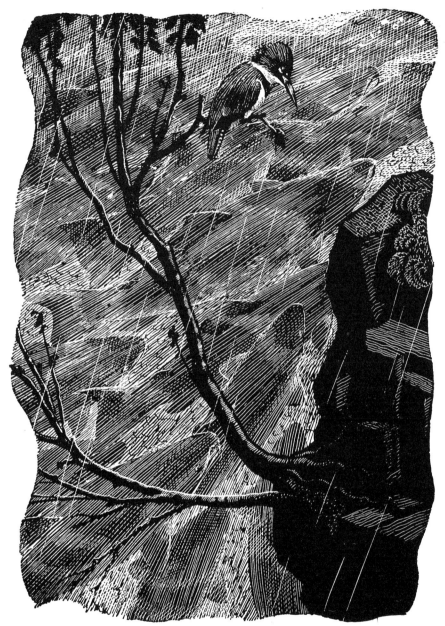

SALMON RETURNING TO SPAWN

*G*reat, red, pale-eyed salmon stared up from its depths; an army passed, phantom-like, underneath. Weary, covered with sores, they shot in from their fight with the stream, rested, and then silently took up their pilgrimage again. Thousands and thousands of salmon, up from the sea, to spawn and then die.

"Ghosts?"

"Aye," said McPherson, "they're ghosts, right enough. Come three weeks every one will be dead."

NEGLEY FARSON

SALMON ENTERING THE RIVERMOUTH

The tide was running. It gurgled among the crannies and beneath the stem of the lighthouse, surging through the channel and among the wooden piles of the docks. She followed it on past the piers and past the bridge, where it spread again over the flats of the inland basin, and so to the east into the womb of the land itself. Within an hour she was in the river enclosed by the marshes on one side and the low meadowland on the other.

This moment was greater than all the moments of her previous life. It was overpowering in its intensity, so that she repeatedly jumped in her excitement.

TERENCE HORSLEY

ASCENDING THE WEIR

Salar swam up on his second attempt; at first he had been unsure of himself, and dropped back almost as soon as he had got a grip on the central cord or spine of water. Swimming again with all his power, he moved slowly into the glissade of water above the white surge, stayed a third of the way up, as though motionless, vibrating; then had gained over the water and swum stronger in jubilation, and suddenly found the sill moving away under him, release of weight from his sides, and calm deep water before him.

HENRY WILLIAMSON

THE FORDING PLACES WERE LOST

A boy had no business to be out when the burn had a froth on it like a glass of stout and the fording places were lost and everything went gliding away, sleek and dangerous as an adder in the long grass.

The sun shone through the rain. I loved the drama of the rain-clouded sky full of great black monsters about to unload gallons of water on the fields.

IAN NIALL

WADING IN FAST WATER

*T*hen the trout fell through a hole in my wretched net. That net was the one thing which wasn't fresh when I began, I had patched it too much in France. Now I was to pay for it.

In my excitement I took my arm from around the supporting pole, stepped forward, as if to catch the fish with my hands, and stepped into a pocket between the boulders. Fish, net, and I started off on our hundred-mile journey to the Atlantic.

NEGLEY FARSON

SALMON, HOOKED

*H*e swam downwards, but could make no progress towards the rock. This terrified him and he turned upwards and swam with all his strength to shake it from his mouth. He leapt clear of the water and fell back on his side, still shaking his head.

HENRY WILLIAMSON

WATCHING BY THE SLUICEWAY

"*H*ullo, hullo! Did 'ee zee that l'il b'uty? My Gor,
'twas a b'tiful sight!"
  *A salmon had leapt out of the white curl-over below
the open fenders, had pierced the green glissade
descending and had swum through, a dark shadow
vanishing.*

HENRY WILLIAMSON

SMALL TORTOISESHELL BUTTERFLIES

The caterpillars of butterflies and moths also feed on plants. They do not, however, suck the sap, but eat the leaves or the wood. This accounts for the very ragged appearance which so many leaves present as the summer advances.

Some of our most beautiful butterflies feed as grubs on the common stinging nettle, namely, the small tortoiseshell, the peacock, the painted lady, the red admiral and the Camberwell beauty. The commonest of them is the small tortoiseshell.

CHARLES S. BAYNE

DRAGONFLY

*W*ith an impulse gentle and elusive, yet vigorous, the insect is
given to the air of which it becomes a part; it dives and lifts,
descending to the rippled surface, then climbing so high with swift
sideway dashes that soon it is lost in the upper blue; soon to return
again and perch quivering in ecstasy.

E. L. GRANT WATSON

GOLDFINCH

The French call this bird by a name derived from the thistle, so notorious has it always been that they live upon this seed. THISTLE is, in French, CHARDON; and the French call this beautiful little bird CHARDONARET. I never could have supposed that such flocks of these birds would ever be seen in England.

The thistles are all cut and carried away from the fields by the harvest; but they grow alongside the roads; and, in this place, in great quantities. So that the goldfinches were got here in flocks, and, as they continued to fly along before me, for nearly half a mile, and still sticking to the road and the banks, I do believe I had, at least, a flock of ten thousand flying before me.

WILLIAM COBBETT

BULLFINCH

WOODCOCK CHICKS

Thither the woodcock led her brood, to probe the mud for worms, flying but a foot above them down the bank, while they ran in a troop beneath; but at last, spying me, she would leave her young and circle round and round me, nearer and nearer till within four or five feet, pretending broken wings and legs, to attract my attention, and get off her young, who would already have taken up their march, with faint wiry peep, single file through the swamp, as she directed.

H. D. THOREAU

WOODCOCK ON THE NEST

A woodcock on the nest is perhaps one of the most charming sights in all nature. The beautifully mottled plumage, the dark velvet bands on the head, and the varying shades of brown and grey on the back, match the surroundings whether of dead leaves or bracken perfectly. The bill itself looks like a dead twig. Only the eyes, those large expressive eyes, black as night, betray the bird to a close observer.

J. W. SEIGNE

CURLEW

WOODCOCK IN FLIGHT

*T*he best ground I ever walked was part of a rough shoot. It consisted of a broad, steep slope covered with rather spindly birch, ash and hazel with occasional clumps of scrub oak. When the ground was hard and the trees stark and bare against that wintry light, I could rely on them rising quickly and giving me next to no chance.

IAN NIALL

THE GROUSE MOOR

WOODCOCK

MAGPIES

*T*o this hedge the hill-magpie comes: some magpies
seem to keep almost entirely to the downs, while others
range the vale, though there is no apparent difference
between them. His peculiar uneven and, so to say,
flickering flight marks him at a distance as he jauntily
journeys along beside the slope. He visits every fir copse
and beech clump on his way, spending some time, too, in
and about the hawthorn hedge, which is a favourite
spot.

RICHARD JEFFERIES

LONG-TAILED TITS

*T*he shaping of the nest at this stage was an amusing sight. The bird would put its head under the dome and keep pushing it up and wriggling from side to side so that the whole nest looked alive.

There was much to be done, and for the next two days there was a great deal of pushing up from the inside, for the dome was inclined to sag, and often it was a struggle to get out. Moss was taken and pushed up from inside into the dome. Soon, however, the main business was the lining of feathers. Even at the very beginning I saw one feather put into the nest and occasionally an odd one was brought afterwards, but when the dome was over feathers were frequently used.

H. F. WITHERBY

BLACKBIRDS

*O*nce we had a crop of Conference, but the Battle of Britain started as they ripened, and the birds had a feast during our temporary evacuation. Now and then a crabbed and miserable Doyenne du Comice managed to survive until September, too crusty and juiceless even for the wasps to eat, and then fell miserably off the tree.

H. E. BATES

THRUSH

THE BIRDS WERE SUFFERING GREATLY

O nce more the blizzards drove through the hedges, piling up into the barbarous, beautiful drifts in the deep southern roads. And again, when the snow had fallen, the wind whipped it off the land in white salt-clouds that in turn piled into finer, sharper drifts. The sky still did not clear, but remained always the colour of a dirty sheepskin. It was now mid-January, and the holly-trees and hawthorns, scarlet and claret only a month before with a million berries, were now stripped black and naked. The birds were suffering greatly. Rooks herded together in oak-trees, holding funereal conferences on the strange state of emergency, sending out only an occasional solitary patrol to survey the land.

H. E. BATES

ROOKS

O bserved in flight or from afar, the rook is a plain black bird. But that does scanty justice to the beautiful colours in his plumage, for so far from being plain black there are four distinct shades of colouring in the bird. His beak and "face" are white, while the crown of his head is a very deep purple-blue, especially deep in the ear-coverts. The feathers on his back are strongly tinted with mauve and bronze, and his tail is dull, almost slate-blue.

G. K. YEATES

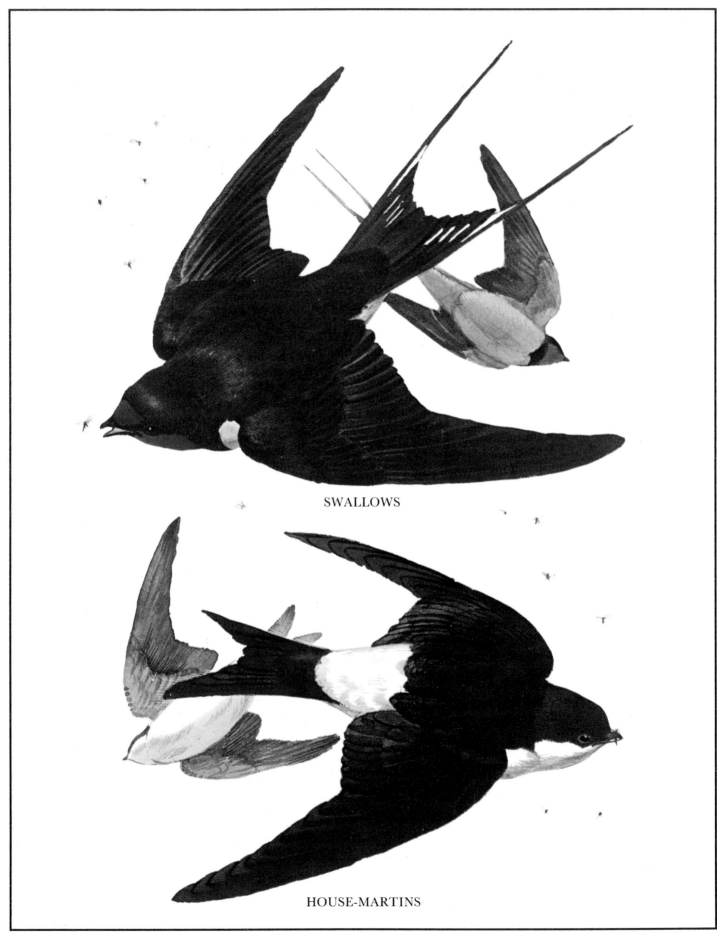

SWALLOWS

HOUSE-MARTINS

SWIFTS

Like the starlings, the swifts have a game which they play regularly with the wildest enjoyment at the end of the day. Instead, however, of being an exercise of skill in manoeuvring as a flock, it is a trial of speed, endurance and skill in the individual. All the members of a colony take part in it, but one volunteers to be hare and the others accept the challenge and set off in pursuit of him. They turn and wheel, swoop and rise, plunge and dash helter skelter round the house, screaming joyously with excitement like a lot of children, then mount high in the air and proceed as before. If the hare is overtaken one of the others sets off in his place, and so the game goes on.

The swifts are among the latest of our summer visitors to arrive, and among the first to go. In the south of England they appear about the first of May, and most of them leave about the middle of August. So they do not have much time for their nesting, and, as the young birds remain in the nest for about a month, they must have only a few days in which to stretch their wings before they start on their long flight to their winter quarters. So the evening game must be invaluable practice for them.

CHARLES S. BAYNE

GANNET (SOLAN GOOSE)

An impression of awe is left on the mind, as one of these great white birds unfolds the vast expanse of its wings, and with the most consummate ease dives into space from the ledge near which you have been standing. Much of impetus there must be in that apparently effortless plunge, or is it merely the weight of its own body which is enough to carry the Solan Goose a quarter of a mile in one long stately curve, before it need use its wings again?

J. H. GURNEY

ALBATROSS

GREAT BLACK-BACKED GULL

The great black-backed gull is a magnificent and beautiful flier. The wing span is that of an eagle, indeed rather larger more often than not, and that, you might think, would necessitate some loss of the grace in the air that is the hall-mark of the gulls. It has meant nothing of the sort. . . .

But you do not find in the great black-back those prolonged wheelings and curvings and circlings that are so characteristic of the herring gull. The bigger bird is more stately and more dignified in the air than it is on the ground, when indeed it has the rather pompous air of the successful business man.

BRIAN VESEY-FITZGERALD

WOODPIGEON

WHERE THE WOODS HANG ON THE HILLSIDES

The pigeon's place as public enemy number one is not in dispute now. It survives so successfully because it feeds on such a variety of food. It takes acorns, ivy berries, wheat, peas, winter cabbage and broccoli of all kinds. It stuffs itself with clover or the bread and cheese of the thorn bush. It is never at a loss even although it must sometimes tax its digestion. The flavour of pigeons varies according to their diet. They are always nice when they have been feeding on stubbles, but ivy berries, which are sometimes their iron rations, hardly improve their flavour! Add to their omnivorous ability the fact that the woodpigeon nests and lays over the longest period of almost any of our native birds and may have young half-fledged in November, or a pair of eggs in the first days of March, and the bird's permanent place in the woods is easily understood.

In recent years I have done a lot of pigeon shooting. Bags in Wales are never particularly high. In this part of the world, where the woods hang on the hillsides, the valleys are small and steep, and the fields only a few acres in size, pigeons tend to be hard to come by and move in comparatively small flocks.

IAN NIALL

SNIPE

*H*er gaze was perfectly steady, and I could not help wondering what was going on in the tiny brain behind that black penetrating eye. It was a direct challenge, almost a duel of will-power.

I was struck by the peculiar attraction which I seemed to have for the bird. It walked very slowly and sedately in my direction, quietly JICK-JACKING as it came, and all the time eyeing me very carefully.

E. C. KEITH

HERONS

Though birds do not perish in great numbers in hard weather, the numbers are covered up in a short time. You would expect it to be severe on such delicate creatures as buntings, woodlarks, skylarks, meadow pipits, wrens, robins and kingfishers, but hardly on such robust species as herons, woodpigeons or plovers. Yet this, again, was quite reasonable when you remembered that, with every pond and lake and many rivers frozen, the food of herons would be almost unobtainable.

H. E. BATES

HERON, FISHING

*W*aiting *for the inhabitants of the pool to settle down again after the slight disturbance that he had made, he surveyed the pool.*

The heron had not fished here very often, as the water was muddy, and it was not easy to see the fish.

For about half an hour the heron stood on one leg, stock-still, as if in deep meditation.

The white morning mists were melting away as the sun came up before he saw anything.

PATRICK RUSS

KINGFISHER

MUTE SWAN

If we were asked to describe the colour of a Swan or a Blackbird, most of us, I think, would answer "white" and "black" respectively. Admittedly this plain description is alright for identification purposes but it is woefully inadequate to describe the true colour of either bird for our purpose of picture making. You will very soon realize that black is not the colour of the Blackbird, especially if the sun is shining on him, and though he is perched among green leaves he is still not black; even in grey winter his blackness is a different quality from that of the dark silhouettes of the bare branches that surround him.

Let us consider what is usually described as the "white" plumage of a fully adult Mute Swan, and the changes it undergoes under varying conditions of light and surroundings. It will not require a great effort on your part to perceive that, in a good light, his plumage is anything but white. Notice the yellow finger in the feathers of neck and upper breast, and the cold bluish purity of the back, wings and tail. Note also the colours of the shadowed under-surfaces, and how it is influenced by the colour of the ground on which the bird is standing; if he is standing on green grass then the under-parts reflect a greenish colour, whereas if he were on dry, golden sand, the reflected colour would be a distinctly warm tint; or, again, if he were flying over water his breast, belly and under-wings would take on a colder tint, especially if the water were reflecting a blue or grey sky.

CHARLES TUNNICLIFFE

GREYLAG GEESE, GRAZING

*T*he little formation flew as one bird over the licking waves, turned, and drove upwind across the beach towards the shoulder of a rounded hill. They knew that this was only an island – had known it in the blackness of the previous night while they were thirty miles away. But the rainwet grass of its arched back offered good grazing, and under the shelter of the hill the gander pitched. For an hour they remained feeding, while the light drained from the sky and a grumble seemed to rise up out of the sea to fill the twilight.

TERENCE HORSLEY

AWAY THEY WENT, AS THOUGH IN SOME SLOW-MOTION FILM

There was another day when the ploughed field was covered in snow that blew like a desert dust storm as a light breeze ran across the land. All at once a long flight of greylags came at hedge height right over my head. Again I did nothing, not from compassion, though I could see every small detail of the geese, their eyes, their tucked-away feet, the upcurve of their pinions as they passed over me, as though in some slow-motion film, but from nothing more than sheer paralysis of mind and body. Away they went, at the same height, across the open field in which I stood like a scarecrow, looking along their backs, experiencing, for a brief second or two, something I could hardly hope to experience again in a lifetime. I am glad now that I didn't put up the gun and look along it to shoot the geese as they flew innocently onwards.

IAN NIALL

GREEN WOODPECKER

GEESE MIGRATING SOUTH

*T*he seven had risen from the edge of a lake which no man had seen for a dozen years, where the willow thickets were dusted with the first fall of winter snow, and the pines thrust spires into an icy silence which was not to be broken for five long months. In that windless dawn, as the last trout had risen to the last spent gnat, and the ice shot its silver stilettos over the black water, they had taken to the wing.

TERENCE HORSLEY

GREYLAG GEESE

*T*he rising of a great flock of geese has something grand about it. There is no arrowing away as with startled duck, no panic flight. Geese have a slower, more powerful take-off. They beat their way up into the air and make a great display of grey and white, something to be remarked for miles around.

IAN NIALL

PEREGRINE WITH PREY, UNDER ATTACK

A speck hung high in the air above her claimed the peregrine's attention; she glanced at it with a swift, sideways motion of her head, and recognized another peregrine.

The tiercel stooped, dashing downwards. She rolled sideways as he approached her, and down he went, spinning a thousand feet before he could check.

PATRICK RUSS

SPARROWHAWK

BARN OWL

*W*hen blanching winter stark and clear
    Silvers the mind with silence white
Till gaudy eye and noisy ear
    Have second hearing, second sight;
When trees are numb as graveyard stones
    And the hard hush nips my marrow-bones

I listen the crisp and tinkling tune
Of water crystalling under the moon –
    The frigid, death-voiced moon.

While cold and sharp and shining sheer
Orion's dagger pricks my ear,
Under an old fir's grizzled cowl,
    Big with his drowsy wide surprise
Wakens the hunched and pawky owl
    And blinks his big moon-marvellous eyes.

JAMES A. MACKERETH

TAWNY OWL

TAWNY OWL

SQUIRREL IN A RAGE

The most irritating squirrel is the one that spots some movement and starts chattering at you. It will go on and on – and on. When it has worked itself up into a nattering, chattering rage it is not easily frightened. You can wave your handkerchief at it, throw your hat in the air or even jump up and down on your seat – actions which will send a normal squirrel scurrying away. But the scolding squirrel will just continue to scold – louder than ever.

ARTHUR CADMAN

OLD BOAR BADGER

LOST, TO ALL APPEARANCE,
IN THE BEAUTY OF RIPPLING WATER

I have seen many a hare enter the water and swim across, when it could just as easily have gone round. The swim was obviously taken to save time and trouble, and was the action of an animal accustomed to this form of exercise. On the Gob, also, you will sometimes see a hare sitting quietly by the water on the landward side, apparently just watching it flow past, lost, to all appearance, in the beauty of rippling water. It will be sitting upright, absorbed (for there is nothing here of which to be afraid; the foxes are only about at night) with great ears laid back.

BRIAN VESEY-FITZGERALD

A RUNNING SHADOW WITH INDISTINCT OUTLINE

The take-off is often a very noiseless affair. They are a wonder blend with their background, brown as the rusted bracken, fawn to match the dead stubbles, the dried-out feather grass, dark on the back so that they look like the blackthorn hedge, rufous on the neck like the red dock leaf. At once they belong to the plough and the stubble, the bracken, the wood and the bank, and their speed is designed somehow to deceive the eye. Perhaps the smoothness of the movement of the running hare is the most camouflaging thing about it. There are times when the creature is a ghost, a running shadow with indistinct outline, and there are times when this fact misleads the man who suddenly becomes aware that he has put one up.

IAN NIALL

STOAT, ALERT

The stoat is a hunter. He preys upon rabbits, rats, mice, birds, and even squirrels, so he may be seen wherever these creatures are to be found. He is very wary. I have seen him pause suddenly and listen when his sharp ears caught the click of a gate a hundred yards away.

CHARLES S. BAYNE

RED SQUIRREL

In the woods we meet with the most charming of all our four-footed animals, the little red squirrel. He is also one of the very few that we may expect to find abroad during the day.

CHARLES S. BAYNE

FOX

*A*s the bracken withers and collapses upon itself, a fox can no longer run through it but must leap in and out. In the autumn, at the fall of the leaf, foxes are more often seen than in summer.

E. L. GRANT WATSON

RED DEER

It is not long before sounds and movements indicate that the forest around is instinctive with life. Often it happens that more may be observed while stationary in one spot than while traversing a mile or two; for many animals crouch or remain perfectly still, and consequently invisible, when they hear a footstep.

RICHARD JEFFERIES

RED DEER ON EXMOOR

*D*og *and I were alone with the water-plashes and the frantic wind-music of the moor. Twenty miles distant a sun-shaft, piercing the discoloration of the storm, lit many fields, travelling fast yet not seeming to move. Shadowy and slim creatures fled away into the mist. What had brought the red deer into the open? Usually they lie "under the wind" among the trees of the coombes, or valleys.*

HENRY WILLIAMSON

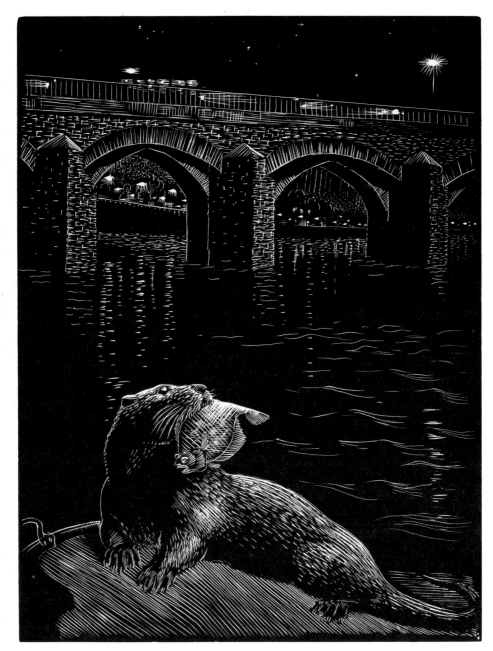

OTTER FEEDING AT NIGHT

This was the first time Tarka passed under the ancient Long Bridge, which the monks built across their ford two centuries before the galleons were laid down in the shipyards below to fight the Spanish Armada. When the otters had passed under the bridge they had to swim hard, keeping near the right bank of the river to avoid the main flow of the tide. Flukes were caught in the estuary that night by the otters diving to deep water; they were not easy to find, for the dabs and plaice lay flat on the sand when they saw the dark shapes above them, and their sandy-speckled backs hid them.

HENRY WILLIAMSON

OTTER WITH CUBS

She climbed on a boulder and lay across it, her head near the stream. She clung by her rudder to the reverse side of the stone, and whistled for the cubs. Tarka had been peering from the holt and, at the first whistle he moved forward into the water, making hardly a ripple.

Behind him swam the cubs, the arrowy ripples pushed from their noses breaking against each other. They followed Tarka across the floating crowsfoot flowers and reached their mother who lay so still. They spoke to her, nuzzling her with their heads and mewing their hunger. When she would not speak to them they bit her rudder, they cajoled and wheedled, they made angry hissing noises but she did not move.

HENRY WILLIAMSON

OTTERHOUND

Huntsman and his whipper-in each lifted a rusty pin from the staples in the back of the van and lowered the flap. Immediately hounds fell out and over each other, and on to the road, shaking themselves, whimpering, panting with pink tongues flacking, happy to be free after the crush and heat of the journey from kennels. They were admired and stroked, patted and spoken to by name; they scratched themselves and rolled and licked each other's necks; they sat and looked up at the many faces.

Deadlock, his black head scarred with old fights, sat on his haunches, apart and morose, watching for the yellow waistcoat of the Master.

HENRY WILLIAMSON

THE OTTERS' HOLT

Soon the pack was trying to break in at the entrance. They did not obey voice, horn and whip at once but had to be urged away . . . .
The Honorary whip, a retired senior officer of the army, prodded with his pole among the roots, and finding soft earth, tried to force the pole to the back of the holt.

HENRY WILLIAMSON

RIDING TO THE MEET

The better class of farmers keep hunters, and ride constantly to the hounds; so do some of the lesser men who "make" hunters, and ride not only for pleasure but possible profit from the sale. Hunting is, to a considerable extent, a matter of locality. In some districts it is one great winter amusement, and almost every farmer who has got a horse rides more or less. In others which are not near the centres of hunting, it is rather an exception for the farmers to go out.

RICHARD JEFFERIES

STAG AT BAY

The watchers on the Ball saw a red speck on a grey horse cantering through the bracken along the farther edge of the wooded goyal. This was the whipper-in, who was to watch where the stag would run. Then they heard the horn faintly singing. So did the stag, where he lay in dread of the return of a fly whose wing-whirr he had just heard – a red-bearded bot-fly that was circling with almost inaudible flight above his head, ready to dart into his nostril, and squirt a drop of fluid containing tiny maggots, which would hook themselves to the skin before he could sneeze out their parent. When he heard the horn he pressed his chin on the ground, and waited. He knew what the horn meant.

A hound whimpered in the wood, but the stag did not move. He listened. The bot-fly settled on the long shaggy hairs of his upper neck, and washed its silver face; for Stumberleap was not breathing. The stag heard the voice of the huntsman, and the more abrupt cries of the whipper-in farther away. . . .

Then a hound threw its tongue, and jumped forward, followed by other tufters. Stumberleap jumped up, and one of his top-points furrowed the bark of a branch above his thrown-up head. One hound made as if to run in upon him, but stopped, remembering.

When the huntsman came up he encouraged hounds with horn and voice, and the ten tongues clamoured about him. Stumberleap kicked at one, and drew from it a yelp of pain. The others pressed upon him, he sank slightly upon his haunches, quivered as he pressed all his strength into his muscles, and sprang over hounds and away among the trees.

HENRY WILLIAMSON

UNTOUCHED BY CIVILIZATION

We talked of the wild nature of such an island that had been deserted by men, and was untouched by civilization, and after a time, my friend went on to speak of what he had named his "philosophy of the fringe".

He maintained that in centres of civilization mankind was withering away. Not that their numbers were getting less (they were obviously increasing), or that they were necessarily physically sickly, though they often were, but that human life was centripetal, having its sources at the circumference, and working inwards towards congestion and death at the centre.

By the circumference he meant such places where we now sat, places, as he put it, on the fringe, where a man could easily feel the initial impulses of life; places where the sky and the ocean and the ungauged forces of the cosmos worked on the open souls of men.

E. L. GRANT WATSON

AUTUMN

There is the mood of calm, of stillness, of completion – and when indeed does the earth seem more at rest than on a windless, October afternoon? Then it seems that all the countryside is sunk in a tranced meditation, with gaze turned inward and backward over the accomplishment of the year, and if we catch the flavour of this calm, we are aware of vague images, like those which flutter between waking and sleep. In this mood we hear the faint rustling of field-mice among grass, and the fainter sound of the hooked feet of the spiders as they stir the fallen leaves; with this mood comes the call of partridges on distant hillsides, or the single line of sound of the buzzing of one belated bee.

As part of the stillness may be counted the subdued bird-voices. The flocks of linnets and finches which flit along the hedgerows, or which spread themselves over the arable, are almost silent; only a faint twittering, which must be listened for. The soft treble of the robin is the only formed and deliberate note that shapes into a song. This song, which grows stronger in the winter, is as yet so sweet and plaintive as but to make more deep the silence. As we yet listen, we can hear the "wailful choir" of gnats as they rise and sink in their prolonged and oft-repeated dances. All these sounds are of that one mood of pause and of anticipation which in the opaque mistiness of an autumn morning makes of every tree an alembic.

E. L. GRANT WATSON

STATIONARY ALL HIS LIFE

Every now and then a difficulty happens in reference to the old green lanes and bridle-tracks which once crossed the country in every direction, but get fewer in number year by year. Sometimes it is desired to enclose a section of such a track to round off an estate: sometimes a path has grown into a valuable thoroughfare through increase of population; and then the question comes, Who is to repair it ? There is little or no documentary evidence to be found – nothing can be traced except through the memories of men; and so they come to the old shepherd, who has been stationary all his life, and remembers the condition of the lane fifty years since. He always liked to drive his sheep along it – first, because it saved the turnpike tolls; secondly, because they could graze on the short herbage and rest under the shade of the thick bushes. Even in the helplessness of his old age he is not without his use at the very last, and his word settles the matter.

RICHARD JEFFERIES

HAWK

The most commanding down is crowned with the grassy mound and trenches of an ancient earthwork, from whence there is a noble view of hill and plain . . . a small swift shadow passes across – it is that of a hawk flying low over the hill.

Some hawks seem always to remain in the meadows; but the majority frequent the arable land, and especially the cornfields on the slopes of the downs, where they may be found in such numbers as rival or perhaps exceed those of any other bird.

RICHARD JEFFERIES

BEEHIVES – SHELTERED FROM THE NORTH AND EAST

In one spot on the edge of the ha-ha is a row of beehives – the garden wall and a shrubbery shelter them here from the north and east, and the drop of the ha-ha gives them a clear exit and entrance. This is thought a great advantage – not to have any hedge or bush in front of the hives – because the bees, heavily laden with honey or pollen, encounter no obstruction in coming home.

How many a man's life has centred about the waggon! As a child he rides in it as a treat to the hayfield with his father; as a lad he walks beside the leader, and gets his first ideas of the great world when they visit the market town. As a man he takes command and pilots the ship for many a long, long year. When he marries, the waggon, lent for his own use, brings home his furniture. After a while his own children go for a ride in it, and play in it when stationary in the shed. In the painful ending the waggon carries the weak-kneed old man in pity to and from the old town for his weekly store of goods, or mayhap for his weekly dole of that staff of life his aged teeth can hardly grind. And many a plain coffin has the old waggon carried to the distant churchyard on the side of the hill.

RICHARD JEFFERIES

FARM WAGGON

TROTTING-HORSE

It wasn't easy to hold him when he brought his forefeet to the road and sprang into the collar, for then he trotted so fast that not only the spokes of the wheels vanished in a blur but his forefeet couldn't be seen either.

He was incapable of breaking the trot. He could neither gallop nor canter. He had the blood of fine trotting-horses in him and the fire that all fast horses need.

IAN NIALL

CLYDESDALE

*M*any a farm child had met with an accident in the
cornfield. Grandfather solved this problem in a
practical fashion by fitting another seat on the binder. I
sailed round with him while the corn was cut, well out of
the way of the great feet of the Clydesdales. I never was
afraid of horses after that, except perhaps ponies. I loved
the draught horse, the magnificent beast that thrust his
great shoulders into the collar and struck the soft earth
with his hind feet as he pounded uphill.

IAN NIALL

GYPSY CARAVAN

The gypsies have come to Kent. The gypsies, the cherry-pickers, with their caravans, their mangy horses, their raucous voices, their cadging habits.

RICHARD CHURCH

THEY CAME BACK IN THE DAWN

That year in the late autumn he was allowed to go with his father and Donald MacDonald, who shared the boat, to set lobster pots in the sea loch. So he learned the meaning of the winter hours. He learned, too, that there was a place forty miles away with a railway, and that the blue lobsters which came out of the green sea went there each day in the van which carried the post, and that the next morning they were hundreds of miles on in London where the King and Queen lived.

In the autumn of the year he was twelve years old, he went into the mountain with his father and came back in the dawn of the following day carrying the quarters of a stag. There was blood on his hands.

"Jamie lad, we'll not speak of this," said his father. The boy understood.

TERENCE HORSLEY

THE VILLAGE COBBLER

In despite of machine-sewn boots and their cheapness, the village cobbler is still an institution, and has a considerable number of patrons. The labourers working in the fields need a boot that will keep out the damp, and for that purpose it must be hand-sewn: the cobbler, having lived among them all his life, understands what is wanted better than the artisan of the cities, and knows how to stud the soles with nails and cover toe and heel with plates till the huge boot is literally iron-clad.

RICHARD JEFFERIES

THE GARDENER

*H*e is sitting in the greenhouse. It is very warm and sunny in the greenhouse and Mr Pimpkins is sitting on a box. The DAILY MAIL *is spread on his knees, and on the* DAILY MAIL *is spread a mountainous sandwich of bread and cheese, a couple of slices of bacon and a large thermos flask of tea. Mr Pimpkins is slowly masticating his way through both the news and the food. You go into the greenhouse, struck instantly by its soft and genial warmth, to remark to Mr Pimpkins, hullo, this is where he is.*

"Jist evvin me breakfast," he says.

H. E. BATES

PASQUE FLOWERS

CHAPTER FOUR

DREAMS AND WONDERLAND

Extracts from

Adventuring with Nomad; Ambush of Young Days; Northwards with Nomad; Out of Doors with Nomad; Over the Hills with Nomad; Plowmen's Clocks; Roving with Nomad; Tales from Ebony; The Country Child; The Farm on the Hill; What to Look for in Autumn; What to Look for in Spring; What to Look for in Summer; What to Look for in Winter.

There was no point in his career when Tunnicliffe decided to illustrate children's country books or sought commissions from publishers in this field. The demand for his services was established from the outset. Alison Uttley's books came, one after another, from 1943 when Faber published *Country Hoard*. This, and the dozen or so that followed, were illustrated with scraperboard. So were the "Nomad" books by Norman Ellison with the imprint of University of London Press. So much of the work Tunnicliffe did for these and the celebrated Ladybird series was so instructive and educational that grown-ups read them with as much delight as their children. A time was yet to come when television would take over in the sphere of natural history, and the public in general would be lured away from the substantial to the ephemeral, from a careful study to a quick flick-through. Writers of these books for children needed just the right balance of illustration. When Alison Uttley wrote about the peaceful country scene, or Nomad took his youthful readers to the high moors, Tunnicliffe drew the butterfly, the bee, or the "windhover" drifting as it searched for a mouse, or something as small as a beetle travelling through the grass. Most children seem to have a natural enthusiasm for the out-of-doors world. They are keen-sighted and, with the right instruction, become very good observers. This pointed the way as far as both author and artist were concerned.

The long collaboration with Alison Uttley was especially successful, as anyone who has read her work will have discovered. There is something of the wondering dreaming child deep inside even the most sophisticated individual, and Alison Uttley's gift was to be able to reach through to this. Charles Tunnicliffe, although he had no children of his own, knew what would please a child, whether it was those workaday horses enjoying their Sunday rest in the shade, someone digging up a Christmas tree, the milk being brought in, or the hay being gathered. In his approach, too, he seemed to have a particular insight, not only into the mind of his author, but those of her readers as well.

WATER VOLE

HILL-FOX

I took the glasses and focused them on the fox, now
barely two hundred yards away. It was a fine specimen
of a hill-fox, larger in the body, decidedly darker in colour,
and with longer legs than the redder and whiter fox of the
lowlands. I wondered if it was the same animal which had
gone to earth amongst the boulders and rocky scree during
the recent fox-drive. Several terriers had been sent in to bolt
it, but Reynard had hidden himself so securely in the maze
of underground runs that the hunt had been called off.

NORMAN ELLISON

BADGERS LEAVING THEIR SETT

B rock, to give the badger his old English name, is really a far commoner creature than is generally supposed. His shy and almost wholly nocturnal habits make him unfamiliar to most people. He is a big fellow — an adult boar will measure thirty inches from nose to root of tail and weigh nearly forty pounds — yet harmless, unless cornered.

NORMAN ELLISON

SWALLOW-TAIL BUTTERFLY

Resting with outspread wings on the white feathery head of a wild-carrot plant was a large butterfly – a swallow-tail. The velvety-black and primrose-yellow latticed pattern of the wings shimmered in the sunlight. We could make out the scalloped edges of the blue-bordered hind-wings: the two projecting "tails" reminded us of the feathered "streamers" of a swallow. This gorgeous insect stayed there for a full minute, slowly opening and closing its wings to the sun.

NORMAN ELLISON

PAINTED LADY AND
SMALL TORTOISESHELL BUTTERFLIES

MARSH HARRIERS – "THE PASS"

*W*ithout warning the hen bird shot out of the reeds, screaming loudly and rose to meet him. As the two came together, we noticed she was appreciably the larger bird. At first I thought she was going to charge into him, but when little more than a yard separated the pair, she turned over almost on her back, shot out her left leg and caught in the outstretched talons the vole dropped by her mate.

"That's what we call the 'pass,'" Harry remarked. "Look, she has gone down in the reeds again. She will be feeding her chicks with that vole now."

NORMAN ELLISON

RAVEN

We peeped over the edge, and there was the hen-raven feeding her newly hatched chicks, unaware that she was being watched by two very curious and interested human beings. We could see three young birds and a single egg which, for some reason, had failed to hatch, and had been kicked to one side of the nest. The youngsters were not particularly handsome in their first suits of mousy-brown down, but the raven was proud of them.

NORMAN ELLISON

THE EYRIE OF THE GOLDEN EAGLE

*W*e counted the bodies of seven grouse partly plucked and dismembered among the debris which littered the platform. Two eaglets crouched there with stumpy wings outspread, gasping in the heat, tormented by the clouds of flies attracted by the dead grouse. One bird was larger than the other and appeared more alert and vigorous; brown feathers were already appearing in patches through its down. The smaller eaglet was still clothed in creamy-white down and seemed to us cowed and timorous. The black-hooked yellow beak was full size, and the yellow talons with black claws looked too large for the body. At this short distance the wide-open eye was keen and fierce, for these were young killers, typical birds of prey.

"They are just five weeks old," Mac informed us, "and I'm hoping both of them will fledge and get away safely. As often as not, the stronger kills the other within the first three weeks."

NORMAN ELLISON

GOLDEN EAGLE IN FLIGHT

BEARDED TITS IN THE REEDS

I suddenly switched on the cunningly concealed lighting
which gave the whole sunlit scene the semblance of reality. . . .
We looked upon a typical Broadland scene on a summer day in June.
Bearded tits, reed-warblers and other birds nested in the screen of reeds
before us; coots and great crested grebes with their families swam in
the water.

NORMAN ELLISON

CRESTED TIT

*A*t last I caught sight of the bird among the thick foliage; a small, restless figure flitting about with the jerky movements of a tit, now hanging upside down, now running up the trunk in the manner of a tree-creeper. Undoubtedly it was a tit of some kind. Then I saw the pointed black-and-white crest – there could be no mistake about that; it was our first crested tit.

NORMAN ELLISON

BITTERN AND YOUNG

GREAT CRESTED GREBE AND YOUNG

In another part of the reed-bed we watched an old grebe swim into an open patch of water with three newly hatched chicks on its back. We thought them delightful little creatures in their first coats of black-and-white striped down. They were snuggled down, warm and comfortable, among the plumage of the broad back, when suddenly the parent bird dived and they were left floating like three buoyant corks. The sudden change evidently did not worry them, for when the old bird surfaced again they quickly climbed back.

NORMAN ELLISON

GUILLEMOT'S EGG

The whole cliff-face reminded me somehow of a tall tenement house of many floors. The top – or roof if you like – was a thick stratum of soil and turf in which the puffins nested. Under the shelter of boulders, and in holes and crevices in the cliff itself, the razorbill crouched on her single egg. At a quick glance it was difficult to distinguish the razorbill from the guillemot, for both had a white shirt-front and a dark tail-coat. (Dick suggested they looked like waiters.) But nearer inspection revealed the deep compressed bill "tied together with a piece of white string," as he so aptly described it, and the much darker upper-parts of the razorbill.

Further down, guillemots crowded the horizontal ledges almost down to sea-level. There was something reptilian in the appearance of these birds as they sat upright, twisting their long sinuous necks this way and that, the large egg held by the webbed feet against the body.

NORMAN ELLISON

THE CROWDED CLIFF-FACE

THE WATER'S EDGE

We returned home by the side of the lovely canal and river, where kingfishers flashed, and where we picked daffodils in early spring. There, too, was a cottage which seemed enchanted to me, for it was built in the wood which dipped down to the water's edge, and the reflection of its ivy-covered walls lay in that tranquil stretch of green water, separated from us by a little swing bridge. Never had I seen a house so close to water, and I associated it with a fairy-tale.

ALISON UTTLEY

A FEW DAYS BEFORE HARVEST

*P*resently the farmer and his son came again to the field and the farmer said, "We can't get our neighbours to help us cut the rye, so to-morrow we will ask our relations to help us."

HARCOURT WILLIAMS

THREE FERRETS, THE COLOUR OF OLD IVORY

There were other helpers who came with the seasons. Eli Bunting, the rat-catcher, visited them twice a year, and brought a load of excitement with him. Work was suspended when he walked through the stile by the big spiked gate into the yard, and stood waiting with his little terrier Jack at his heels for the frantic barking to bring someone out.

He opened his bag and held up three ferrets, the colour of old ivory. They shot their long flat heads sideways and stared with their pink eyes at the little crowd that gathered.

ALISON UTTLEY

LIKE A PICTURE OF DON QUIXOTE

The pig-sticker rode to the big white gate, he leaned forward to unlatch it, and then he dismounted. He wore a white smocked frock, girded with a leather belt in which was tucked a long knife which he fondled and stroked with his gnarled, dirty fingers. His smock was kilted high for riding, and on his head he wore a wide-brimmed hat of felt. He was like a picture of Don Quixote, except that his nag was fat and the knight's was bony.

ALISON UTTLEY

THE ROOKERY

*I*n early March the buds of elm trees are swelling, and rooks are gathered in their rookeries and are rebuilding the nests of last season. Each pair is particular about its own nest, and seems to know and be able to identify every twig. Sometimes a rook will steal a twig from another nest when the rightful owners are absent. The theft is soon discovered; there is a great rumpus, and much cawing and scolding until the missing stick is found.

In the distance a flight of rooks is mobbing a solitary heron. A heron standing his ground can use his great dagger of a beak far better than he can use it when in flight.

E. L. GRANT WATSON

THE SWALLOW TRIBE

*B*y early September the swifts have already migrated to warmer climates, and the swallow tribe begins to gather on roof-ridges and telegraph wires in readiness for their migration.

The swallows can be distinguished from the martins by their reddish-chestnut throats and foreheads, their beautiful steel-blue backs and wings, and their long, forked tails. The house martins have short tails, black backs; are white beneath from chin to tail, and have very noticeable white rumps. The sand-martins – which are the smallest of the three – have dark brown backs, white underparts – with a brown band across the breast, and no white rump.

E. L. GRANT WATSON

HE BROUGHT HIS OLD WAYS WITH HIM

The print bonnets hung behind one of the doors in the kitchen, and when I was three or four a smock frock belonging to old Josiah hung there too. He was an old man who lived with us for many years, and he brought old ways with him, such as my father had known in his youth. He wore a smock frock of coarse white linen, handwoven by his wife, with elaborate work across the front. When he went milking he put this on, to keep his clothes clean, and very delightful I thought it was, although I was surprised to see an old man in a pinafore.

ALISON UTTLEY

BRINGING IN THE MILK

Outside was the deep spacious night. The interior of the room was reflected on the window, but by pressing her face against the pane Susan could see the cowhouses. A little glimmer moved across the cow-yard, and then another star joined it. The two lights bobbed and bowed as if talking together, and then they moved in dancing rhythm like spectral will-o'-the-wisps one behind another across the field path. The men were returning with their brimming milkcans, walking slowly to keep the milk from spilling, swinging the lanterns by their pails.

ALISON UTTLEY

WEASEL

*T*he prickly seed-shucks of the chestnut have fallen and burst open, some of them spilling the brown 'conkers' out of the smooth, soft linings that have contained and nourished them.

A weasel, with its paws on a large root which stretches from the chestnut trunk, has just knocked down one of the wood-blewit toadstools. A weasel can easily kill a bird as large as a hen, and even a full-grown rooster. It is the enemy of all gamekeepers, as it sucks the eggs of both partridge and pheasant. On the other hand, it might be considered to be the farmer's friend, for it kills large numbers of field-mice.

E. L. GRANT WATSON

THE FOREST FLOOR IN MAY

*B*etween the white dead-nettle and the blue bugle blossoms is a half-hidden partridge's nest.

The wild arum (sometimes called cuckoo-pint or lords-and-ladies) is a strange plant. Within the pale-green expanding sheath the upper part of the spadex is a dark-purple or pale pink. This spadex has a temperature rather higher than the surrounding air, and also a peculiar smell. Flies are tempted to come and warm their feet, and then crawl down the spadex past a ring of short threads which prevent them from crawling back.

E. L. GRANT WATSON

THEY WHEELED ROUND AND TORE BACK AGAIN

Every year, for two hundred years at least, lambs ran the same race in Whitewell field. In other fields they had their odd games, but here it was always the same.

By the side of one of the paths stood the oak tree, with the seat under it, and a short distance away stood the great spreading ash. The lambs formed up in a line at the oak, and at some signal they raced to the ash, as fast as their tiny legs would go; then they wheeled round and tore back again.

ALISON UTTLEY

THE DAY OF REST

*O*n *Sundays we walked if we wanted to go anywhere. It was the day of rest for the horses, and they stood in the fields, the church bells ringing in the valley below, in the certain knowledge they wouldn't be needed after the milk was taken to the station.*

ALISON UTTLEY

JUST IN TIME

*T*hunder-clouds have darkened the northern sky. In the foreground, sunshine is still bright on the bramble flowers, the foxglove and the pink campion. From the clouds a fork of lightning flashes to earth, and nearby the thunder crackles. The farmer is just in time to stretch his tarpaulin and keep the rain from his newly-stacked hay.

The clouded-yellow butterfly that is flying near the bramble will have to seek shelter if it is not to be beaten down by heavy rain – and possibly drowned.

E. L. GRANT WATSON

SUMMER NIGHT

*H*edgehogs, slugs and moths are all night-feeding creatures. A car has been
stopped, and the headlights illumine the side of the road, showing the woodland
margin and penetrating into the depths of the woods beyond. The hedgehog has
"frozen" in sudden alarm. It is on its nightly rounds looking for slugs and insects
and, indeed, any small creature that its sensitive nose can smell out and its little,
sharp teeth can crunch up. In a moment the hedgehog will gather up courage and
proceed on its way, and then no doubt it will gobble up the two slugs.

E. L. GRANT WATSON

GATHERING THE HAY

*W*hen a cart was piled with a mountain of hay, ropes were thrown over to keep the load from slipping off as the mares struggled to the stack-yard.

"Pull! Pull! Pull agen! Pull agen! Agen! And agen! And agen!" sounded through the summer air like a sea-chanty as the Irishmen strained at the ropes to tighten the mass. Then the man on the top slid down and the perilous ascent began.

Other men hung like flies on one side to keep the top-heavy load from tumbling over and falling down the field. It was always an anxious time, a slip and a man and mare might be killed.

ALISON UTTLEY

ITS SPLENDOUR WAS NOT MISSED

*T*he sky was scrutinized as if it were an
illuminated missal with pictures of angels and
rainbows and round-faced cherubs with wide-open
mouths blowing for the wind. Its splendour was not
missed, for there was always somebody on the watch
for events up there. We had an admiration and
reverence for the heavens with their fantastic ever-
changing clouds by day, their shooting stars by night,
and never a night passed without the little gold
meteorites rolling like marbles over the sky. They seem
to be visible to some people, while others miss them.

ALISON UTTLEY

THE SHEEP FOLD

*A*n *afternoon scene shows a shepherd who has folded his sheep in a large pen, built of hurdles and stakes. The sheep have been gnawing at the roots of the swedes, and have nibbled most of them down to earth level. They are young ewes of this year, and in good condition. To-morrow, or the next day, when they have eaten the roots down to the tap-root, the shepherd will put up another pen, taking in part of the green field beyond – where other swedes are growing, and will drive in his sheep to eat down another patch.*

The shepherd is looking up at an exceptionally large skein of whooper swans which has come from colder climes, probably from Russia.

E. L. GRANT WATSON

MUTE SWANS

*A*utumn, with its heavy rains, has filled the pond to the brim, and has flooded the track to the farm. In his raincoat and gum-boots the cowman is walking on the drier part away from the wheel tracks which are so full of water.

A female mute swan (called by swan-breeders, a 'pen') has come with three cygnets to see what can be found among the tangle of flag-leaves that fringe the pond. The cygnets still have the grey down of their first year, but now – in late autumn – white feathers are beginning to appear on their scapulars. Mute swans are misnamed, for they are not mute, but can give loud grunts of indignation when they think themselves to be threatened.

E. L. GRANT WATSON

THE MORNING AIR WAS SWEET

Steps were approaching across the grass, the garden gate banged and Mrs. Garland hurried down the path. She stooped to pick some thyme and a bunch of parsley bordering the stones. Then she sighed deeply and went out again.

Susan sat very still. She looked up at the sky. The morning air was sweet with the smell of the great woods which were only a few yards away, over the wall and across a dell.

ALISON UTTLEY

THE SWING

The swing had its dangers, and I was badly hurt more than once, for the ground was rocky, and the swing was not for a child. There was a legend that a servant boy had once swung so high that he had touched the great outstretched bough of the oak with his feet. Everyone who came to our famous swing tried to emulate him, but I never saw it done. We flew to dazzling heights, sitting on Patty's knee, when a farm man pushed, but there was a breathless terror in the experience. However, when the creaking groan of the chain told of this strain, someone would come to the door and signal angrily for us to stop.

ALISON UTTLEY

BARN OWL

A *full harvest moon is rising, though it is still only twilight. Farm buildings, ricks and church tower are still easily seen in the half-light, so also is the barn owl on its perch – on the look out for mice or any small birds that have not yet gone to roost. An owl's eyes are even bigger than they appear, for the larger part of the eyeball is concealed within the skull. These eyes can see exceedingly well in twilight.*

The wayfaring tree on the right is not truly a tree, but a large, branching shrub. It is a beautiful plant, and one wonders how it got its romantic name.

In the foreground is traveller's-joy – another romantic name! Notice its feathered seeds, which will remain through the winter and fall in the spring.

E. L. GRANT WATSON

THE THAW

*T*he soil has thawed sufficiently to allow the farmer to start ploughing. He is sitting on his tractor that draws the four-furrow plough, and is glancing back at the gulls that follow to pick worms out of the upturned earth.

A flock of lapwings is circling to come down and join in the feast. They have a flickering flight, made particularly noticeable by their broad, black and white wings. Some rooks have already settled on the furrows beside the gulls.

Nearby a hare is running across the furrows and the strip of unploughed field. His greater size, and the dark tips to his long ears, easily distinguish him from a rabbit. Some snow is still lying on the distant hillside.

E. L. GRANT WATSON

MOONLIGHT

Upstairs, downstairs, in pantry, parlours, and dairy, ran little candles all the winter evenings, like glow-worms in the dark. They even went out of doors, sheltered in curving hands, when Becky went to the trough or Dan fetched the milk. When the lanterns were blown out, after milking, candles were used for everything, except when the moon was out to do his share of work....

She crept from her bed and looked out of the window. A soft radiance flooded the fields making them white as snow.

ALISON UTTLEY

THE GROUND HAD BEEN LIKE IRON

In the middle of the table was a Christmas tree, alive and growing, looking very much surprised at itself, for had not Tom dug it up from the plantation whilst they were at church, and brought it in with real snow on its branches. . . .

The ground had been like iron, the tree had spreading roots, but they had not harmed the little thing, and it was going back again to the plantation when Christmas was over.

ALISON UTTLEY

THE EVENING FLIGHT

A red sunset on a frosty evening promises fine weather to come. Starlings are flying in converging flocks towards their roosting place in the trees beyond the lake. Already some are perching in the upper branches, but most of the flocks are slow to settle, and for a long while swoop to and fro, making curious patterns. Separate flocks are meeting to divide again, and all the while more birds will be alighting in the tree-tops. Their chatterings can be heard from far away, and so can the whirring of their passing wing-beats. As they settle they talk loudly in their starling language.

Magpies also gather together in winter and early spring at roosting-time; sometimes seven or eight together; at other times as many as thirty or more.

E. L. GRANT WATSON

OUT HUNTING BY DAYLIGHT

*S*now has been falling for several days, and even in the woods it has covered all the ground. The rabbits can find no grass to eat, and so to still their hunger are gnawing the bark from young beech trees.

The deep footsteps in the snow show the marks made by their larger hind feet. A fox also has passed this way; from his tracks one can see that he was running: two footmarks, one in front of another, then a gap, then two more.

A barn owl, who is no doubt hungry, since most of the mice are under the snow, is out hunting by daylight, hoping for some unwary small bird or a mouse who has ventured out to smell the upper air.

E. L. GRANT WATSON

ARCTIC TERN'S NEST

ROSEATE AND COMMON TERNS

ROSEATE TERN

FOOD BEGGING

COMMON TERNS

IMMATURE BLACK-HEADED GULLS

INDUCING PARENT TO REGURGITATE

LITTLE TERNS MALE POSTURING

CHAPTER FIVE

THE CALL OF THE WILD

Extracts from
Shorelands Summer Diary

One of the advantages of being a writer or an artist is that the person who has opted for either of these professions may choose where he settles. For the writer it is sometimes to his advantage to be distanced from his subject and benefit from significant recall. The artist will refresh his impressions and sometimes benefit from having his subjects on his very doorstep. There was certainly a feeling that to live close to his subjects was essential when Tunnicliffe took his wife on a holiday to the island of Anglesey; for it was at around this time that some of his field work on the Cheshire meres was being culled for *Mereside Chronicle*, the book we have reserved for our final encore. The happy couple fell in love with the place. It had everything, it seemed; a farmland landscape, distant mountains, seacliffs, strands on the tidelines where waders trilled and cleeping oyster-catchers worked over wet seaweed. More than this, on the mouth of the Cefni estuary, at a sleepy Welsh village called Malltraeth, there was a house, tucked away, but not a stone's throw from the shore. It seemed "the stuff that dreams are made on" and Charles Tunnicliffe, after he had reconnoitred the place from a respectable distance, hastened to make the acquaintance of the proprietor of the nearby Joiners Arms. He persuaded the landlord to get in touch with him if and when that quiet house on the shore came up for sale.

Soon after their holiday the Tunnicliffes received the news they had hoped for, and lost no time in buying their dream. *Shorelands Summer Diary*, a masterpiece, was the result of that decision. It is not only an account of the move and the conversion of a room into a studio but of the dream coming true as Tunnicliffe sat behind his window and watched the seabirds come in and go back with the tide. Here were all the waterfowl he could ever have wished for, and more besides, shags fishing from the rocky outcrops, peregrines at South Stack, the hawks and owls he drew so well; rarities that kept him out field sketching in sun and shower, summer and winter. Often he was out sketching for as much as ten hours at a time; after which he would drive himself to catch up with other important items, commissions, and deadlines for advertisers. Rarely did the Tunnicliffes go away and leave this wonderful place. When they did it was almost invariably to gather further reference, to get closer to the elusive bittern or the dainty, shy avocet. More than half Tunnicliffe's working life was to be spent here. Both he and his wife ended their days at Shorelands and *Shorelands Summer Diary*, an account of a single season, could be called the summer time of their lives. It was beautifully produced by Collins with sixteen colour plates and 185 vignetted scraperboards; and it has become a much-prized collector's piece for those who appreciate this particular fragment of Tunnicliffe's life's work.

THE WINDING LANE TO THE HOUSE

On the evening of March the 27th, my wife and I crossed over Telford's great bridge which spans the Menai Straits, and entered the island county of Anglesey. We were no strangers to this fair country, but our journey to-day was different from all previous ones for, at the end of it, in a little grey village at the head of an estuary, there was an empty house which we hoped to call home as soon as we could get our belongings into it. Our other visits had been short holidays, spent chiefly in watching and drawing birds and landscape of which there was great variety. Several sketch-books had been filled with studies of Anglesey and its birds, and we had been specially delighted to find that the island in spring and autumn was a calling place for many migratory birds, while summer and winter had their own particular and different species. Occasionally, to add to the excitement, a rarity would appear. Whatever the season there were always birds and this fact had greatly influenced us in our choice of a new home.

CHARLES TUNNICLIFFE

ANGLESEY FARMLAND

SHOVELLER DRAKES

FOEL FERRY

After a day of work indoors we went out in the evening and found ourselves eventually gazing over the Menai Straits from the road which skirts the shore at Foel Ferry. The tide was low and the sandbanks of the straits were uncovered as also were the mussel beds and shingle stretch of the near shore. We saw that there were birds on the mussel beds but, for the moment, we were distracted by the grandeur of the mountain panorama in front of us. From the quarried sides of Penmaen Mawr in the east to the peaks of Yr Eifl in the west the great hills stood, beautiful in the evening light, their shoulders and precipices dappled by cloud shadow. Snowdon was cloud-capped and in gloom all the time. Across the water, to the south-west, Caernarvon town lay, sometimes in golden sunlight, sometimes in shade, and it was remarkable how frequently the castle alone was sunlit while the rest of the town was shadowed by cloud. But our real objective was birds, and glasses and telescope were at length lowered to a more terrestrial angle where they at once picked up Oystercatchers on the mussel beds, with Curlew and Redshank. I was anxious to see just how the Oystercatcher dealt with mussels, and concentrated on one bird which was most active among the shells.

CHARLES TUNNICLIFFE

CAERNARVON CASTLE

SWALLOWS ON THE HOUSE ROOF

Today the swallows came to the house. They came in hundreds, twittering excitedly all about the roof and the garden, and in the afternoon the slates of the roof as well as the ridge tiles were populated with them as they basked in the bright sunlight. Many were young birds, but there were a few long-tailed, chestnut-throated adults with them. W. and I agreed that we had never seen a more exquisite sight than this. On the warm slates some of them rested on their sides with one wing and tiny foot turned skywards as if revelling in the warmth. Others preened vigorously, and some young birds crouched and asked for food whenever a flying bird approached them, even when that flying bird was a young one like themselves. Many times I saw tiny morsels of food passed from an adult to a young one while they were on the wing. Tirelessly they flew around the chimney-stacks, over the garden, and over the sands where some, for a moment, rested before again joining the excited throng.

CHARLES TUNNICLIFFE

HARRIER HUNTING BY BONT FARM FIELD POOL

ROSEATE TERNS

SHAG AND NESTLINGS

ARCTIC TERNS

A dreadful day! Winds which threatened to blow everything across the island and a high tide at noon, made all other gales we have experienced here seem infantile. At its height great spouts of spray came over the garden wall, sometimes in solid jets, at others in wide clouds of fine spray which enveloped the end of the nearest little cottage, the yard of which was awash. On the lawn a wide pool developed, and another on the drive, both of which were caused by spray and not rain. We were pleased when "high tide" was past but, owing to the following south-west gale, it was several hours before the sand of the estuary became uncovered. Across the wet expanse the swollen river rolled, and, to-day, the lovely S-bend was obscured by the brown flood water.

In the evening I went along the road between the field pools and Cob Lake. Over both sheets of water terns were feeding. Their numbers had increased considerably since yesterday, and in the two companies, there must have been about sixty birds. To-night it was a real fairy ballet, an elegant performance of dipping, soaring, flickering dancers, with the hissing waves as their stage and a scurrying wind-torn sky as backcloth.

CHARLES TUNNICLIFFE

SOUTH-WEST GALE

*T*o the east a rainbow shone against a dark thundercloud which had slowly formed among the mountains and which now enveloped them completely. Against this dark blue cloud the nearer landscape blazed with yellow light, and the shadows of gables and house-sides were almost black and very distinct. On came the cloud, and, as we checked to watch its progress across the vista of marsh, the first heavy drops of rain hit the car. Bodorgan and the village were still sunlit when a flight of birds wheeled over the Cob and, after some manoeuvring, moved down the lake in a close, dark formation and, after more turns and undecided flutterings, alighted on mud at the lower end. We turned and went back after them, and found them to be Whimbrel, a charming company of thirty-four. They preened on the mud spit under the shadow of the Cob, with Dunlin and Redshank for company.

CHARLES TUNNICLIFFE

WHIMBREL ARRIVING OVER COB LAKE

DRAKES FIGHTING

BLACK-TAILED GODWITS FIGHTING

WELSH BLACK CATTLE ON BONT FARM POOL

*A*ll the weather signs seemed to indicate "Set Fair" this fine morning. When I went out to the river for a dip the mountains were only faintly visible through the sunlit haze. By the widening river Herons, Gulls, and Cormorants rested. No bird called and all was quiet over the vast expanse of the estuary. Away out at the bar, three miles distant, there was already a shimmer of heat, and birds on the far sand-bank seemed to be resting in mid-air. By mid-morning the heat had increased so much that I was glad enough to work indoors. From the upper windows I could see the black cattle standing in the shallow and diminishing water of Cob Lake and the field pools, and, among them, a flicker of small birds which proved to be young Pied Wagtails and Starlings feeding on the soft mud. The Swifts have moved on, and after a careful search with the glasses only two were discovered flying about the lake. Not for several years have the island farmers been granted such weather for the hay harvest and, on the high ground on both sides of the marsh, the cleared fields show palely in the chequer-board pattern of pastures and rough land.

This is the time of holiday visitors and, to-day, they were making the most of the weather. Scattered along the grassy length of the Cob little groups of visitors lazed in the warm sun, or ventured across the sands and into the shallows of the river intent on bathing. To-day there were few shrieks as the bathers entered the water for it, too, was warm.

CHARLES TUNNICLIFFE

HOT DAY ON THE COB

STACKING AT PARC WALL

*T*he countryside was full of colour. Beyond the grey stone walls bordering the road lay great stretches of stubble awaiting the plough, and on these golden fields flocks of geese were foraging. Geese seem to have done well on the island for there are flocks everywhere, and it is to be hoped that a local proverb "Good for feather, bad for wool", has not been fulfilled this year. Certainly there seems to be a goodly number of sheep also.

The stackyards were full of hay and corn, and there were some pretty examples of the local thatchers' art which, at its best, is as neat and workmanlike a job as any stack-thatching I know. It has to be efficient for the winds of Anglesey are merciless and search out all slip-shod work. About the stacks and farmyards wandered droves of turkeys, scratching and pecking here and there, enjoying their brief life.

CHARLES TUNNICLIFFE

ANGLESEY THATCHING

FALCON FEEDING YOUNG

THE FEMALE EYESS

I felt that I must make an effort to visit the Peregrines on South Stack cliffs so, after working indoors all morning, I was glad to be, by mid-afternoon, on the flowery edge of the great headland. My pleasure was increased when I focused the glasses on the Peregrine's nest, for there was the falcon, in a good light, feeding two well-grown nestlings from a gory mess held under her talons. She glared across at me for several seconds, then bent her beautiful head and neck and resumed her vigorous pulling, straining against the resistance of her steel-strong legs to tear fragments of flesh from the corpse, which she gave to the young birds. Soon they appeared satisfied, and the falcon, changing her position so that she faced outwards, moved her prey which I now identified as a Puffin. Its orange legs stuck up from the torn body and a few feathers floated on to the growth of sea-pinks at the nest edge which was now untidy and streaked with white. The falcon stood gazing seawards, her own crop full and bulging, then, gripping the remains of the Puffin, she left the nest and sailed down the cliff with the prey dangling from one foot. She disappeared below the edge of the cliff on which I was sitting and I turned my attention to the two nestlings which were moving aimlessly about the nest hollow. One was considerably larger than the other; both were still covered with grey-white down but the beginnings of feathers could be discerned at the centre breast and the wing edges. Presently one staggered to the edge of the nest, turned its "tail" seawards, and evacuated in a white jet over the edge.

My gaze, wandering over the area of cliff near the nest, discovered the falcon perching quietly on a beautiful clump of sea-pink about seven feet from the nest. I had not seen her return to the cliff. She looked very comfortable, matronly, and dignified as she sat there.

CHARLES TUNNICLIFFE

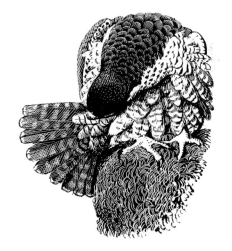

CLEANING HER TOES

FALCON PREENING

*T*he *falcon rose on her feet and began to call, then turned round gripped the Puffin remains and flew with it round the cliff. A minute later she was back and made her perch on a clump of thrift near the nest. Here she called again but no tiercel answered. She moved on to the crest of the round thrift cushion and, stooping, wiped her bill first on one side then on the other. She then returned to the edge, perched and continued with her toilet.*

CHARLES TUNNICLIFFE

PEREGRINES' DOMAIN

Hearing that there was to be a parade of Shire Stallions at Llangefni to-day, and being keen to revive old memories of similar parades in East Cheshire, W. and I went to town this afternoon, and found it full of people and cars. Farmers and their wives, sons and daughters were in the majority and the long main street was full of their quick Welsh speech. Some of the farmers were purposefully making their way up the hill which leads from the centre of the town so, following in their footsteps we came eventually to a field in which was a roped enclosure lined with spectators. Inside the ropes were the stallions and their grooms, and when we arrived a black stallion with white legs was showing his paces. Proudly he trotted down the centre of the enclosure, neck arched, "feathers" streaming, ribbons waving to his movements. At the ropes the groom turned him and trotted him back again, and at the far end came to a halt by the ropes. In the centre of the open space stood a man with a card, who, as the next stallion came down the grass, shouted out its name and other details of the animal. This stallion had fine action and, when it began to trot, there were exclamations of approval from the farmers. The stallion covered the course in grand style. Just as stylishly his little groom pranced by his side, and it was difficult to say which lifted knees the higher – stallion or groom.

CHARLES TUNNICLIFFE

STALLION PARADE

MONTAGU'S HARRIER AND ARCTIC TERNS

LLANDDEUSANT MILL

*P*ast the little white cottages and the grey farmhouses we went; past the little grey churches with their tiny bell towers at the west gable, and the old sail-less towers of windmills (plain evidence of the amount of corn which must have grown in Anglesey's fertile soil years ago), until we came to Llanddeusant where there is a windmill, the only one on the island I believe, which still retains its sails. There it stood, on high ground to the west of the village, its four great arms fixed and immovable, and the slats of the sails hanging loose and derelict, the playing perches of Jackdaws and the look-out posts for Kestrel and Carrion-crow. Daylight showed through the curved timbers of the roof, through which the weather penetrates to the interior timbers, hastening their decay and destruction.

CHARLES TUNNICLIFFE

HARRIER TEARING ITS PREY

HERON WITH AN EEL

*H*e moved and struck seven times before bringing to light his prey – a large eel which writhed and twisted, wrapping itself around the bill, its tail at times beating the herons forehead and crown. However there was no escape and, stepping carefully through the shallows to the shore, the heron walked with slow deliberate strides up the grassy slope of the Cob until he reached the top and his shape appeared against the sky.

CHARLES TUNNICLIFFE

ADULT AND YOUNG HERONS

ESTUARY AT SUNSET

Tea finished, we reluctantly turned the car, and soon we were climbing to the wild uplands behind the bay, by a little road which was new to us. From this high ground it seemed as if the whole of Anglesey lay below us, mile upon mile of rolling country dotted about with grey farms and little white cottages, away to Caernarvonshire and its great blue mountains in the south and east. Slowly we travelled home, the warm light of the setting sun mellowing the grey stone walls and farms, and turning into a veritable blaze the orange-lichened roofs of barn and byre. Westward the sun was sinking between lines of red and purple cloud whose edges were aflame with golden light, and when we reached the sea again near Rhosneiger its waves were a deep purple tipped with rose and gold. The sun went down red behind a purple haze of cloud which lay on the horizon. Land and sea became shadowed, all except the mountains which, as they caught the last of the light, took on the most delicate lilac tint. Slowly the shadows crept up their flanks until only Snowdon's peak was lit, and gradually it, too, lost the rosy light and became a blue silhouette against an almost green sky.

In the deepening twilight we reached home and, before going indoors, gazed down the length of the estuary. We still find it difficult to believe that we really live and work in this place so close to the birds and the sea. However, there they were, the great white drifts of gulls just discernible on the darkening sands, the calling of unseen Curlew, and the distant roar of the breakers at the bar.

Low over the house a formation of belated gulls passed, their white undersides catching the last of the afterglow, and as they disappeared in the dusk we unlocked the door and lit the lamps, feeling well content.

CHARLES TUNNICLIFFE

191

THE FOOTBRIDGE OVER THE OUTLET STREAM, REDESMERE

CHAPTER SIX

BELOVED COUNTRY

Extracts from
Mereside Chronicle

Apart from cherished memories of childhood, preserved in his sketches of the village and farm at Sutton Lane Ends, Charles Tunnicliffe confirmed a distinct environmental inspiration in the later stages of his life. He could not return to the farm after his studies at the Royal College because it had been sold, so he had gone to live in nearby Macclesfield. He had married his first love, who supported him in everything he did and worked as a teacher of art and craft herself; while he threw himself into frenzied activity as a freelance commercial artist. At the same time he was doing book illustration and taking the first steps towards bird portraiture. It was as a by-product of his field work, sketching birds, that *Mereside Chronicle* came about. Before this Tunnicliffe had gone to the canal banks, to sketch and draw subjects that were in the main scenic and as near to landscape as he would ever get. But the Cheshire meres were something different. They were not just escape from the unexciting background of the housing estate and the treeless avenue in which he lived. They were the haunt of waterfowl, the natural scene in which the grebe or the swan swam in open water and nested in the reeds. The young artist had acquired a motorbike and took himself off, whenever he got the opportunity and deadlines with his advertising agency would permit, to sketch at Bosley Reservoir, Gawsworth, Radnor, Siddington and Capesthorn. His first concern was to collect sketches of the various species for reference; until one day he realized he had a full record of the bird life of the meres and pools; with all the seasonal changes and their effect on the birds and their surroundings. Encouraged by *Country Life*, he increased the number of his visits and completed a kind of diary of a twelve month, *Mereside Chronicle*, which delighted his fans when it was published in 1948. Quite plainly a part of it, dealing with Tunnicliffe's visits to the highlands of Scotland, was a kind of make-weight; but nevertheless it in no way detracted from the quality of the whole. The book contained no less than 207 illustrations, plus pages of maps, and a dust jacket which was, like the rest of the work, in monochrome. The work of the mereside was part of Charles Tunnicliffe's beloved native country, a scene to which he was irresistibly drawn while he lived in what was, for him, a dreary suburban atmosphere.

BLACK-HEADS ON THE ICE

Yesterday's frost must have been very keen, for it had frozen the whole of Redesmere from end to end. The snow had ceased to fall, but in the north, the heavy grey sky held a threat of more to come, and a leaden haze hid the far shore.

Forty yards from the road a small flock of Black-headed Gulls stood or squatted on the ice. How different was their appearance against the pure white of their surroundings! Gone was the usual impression of pearly-grey and dazzling white which they gave when seen against a snow-less landscape: instead they looked dusky grey, some-what untidy, and most uncomfortable.

TUFTED-DRAKE FROZEN TO THE ICE

The south end of the reservoir was without a trace of bird-life; no Grebe, no Duck. I was turning away, and about to retrace my steps along the path, when I thought I detected a movement at the edge of the opposite shore, where the snow-covered stones of the built-up bank were reflected in a large patch of open water. The glasses revealed a Tufted drake sitting on a shelf of ice which was slightly higher than the level of the water, the bird most difficult to see against the white of the snow and black of the stones. It sat there without movement save for quick turns of its head. I whistled at it, and threw my arms about, but it did not move. Then I kicked stones out of the frozen bank and shied them towards it, but still it did not budge.

So I took the path again and went round the end of the water to reach the opposite shore. From the top of the steep bank I could see the drake below me, a beautiful bird with snowy white flanks and a long crest. It stared wildly at me with its yellow eye, but still did not move. Then I started to climb down to it, and had almost reached it, when, with a short struggle and a break of ice, it flopped into the water, swam for a few yards with its neck and head carried low, then took to wing.

CHARLES TUNNICLIFFE

THE PATH AND FEEDER UNDER SNOW

When I arrived at Bosley I found that the snow had fallen more heavily there than at Capesthorne. Where the lanes lay below the level of the fields the blizzard had filled them with long, deep drifts which stretched from hedge to hedge. Every tussock of grass, clump of rush, and upward-growing plant and tree had its buttress of snow.

By the reservoir a frozen quietness reigned, and there was no sign of life anywhere on the white landscape. The tops of the hills were hidden in a leaden-grey fog.

COOT PROCESSION IN THE SNOW

By the base of a big oak-tree which grew in the pasture a flock of Coot sat on the snow, while at the other side of the tree eleven Partridge squatted. When the Partridge made an abrupt departure the Coot by the oak-tree root rose to their feet, and started to walk to the pool, a grotesque, funereal procession. Their big feet were lifted high as they stepped laboriously over the snow, and when they had but a few more yards of pasture to cover they took wing, and fluttered on to the pool to make an unfortunate landing where the snow lay three inches deep. They tried to walk through it, floundering and falling on to their breasts, until finally some gave up and sat where they had fallen, as if too exhausted to go on. How miserable and ill-adapted they seemed in this hard weather.

CHARLES TUNNICLIFFE

GREBE DISPLAY – FIRST POSITION

A gentle rain had begun to fall when over the water came the harsh, guttural call of a Great Crested Grebe, and presently the bird broke surface just beyond the fringe of reeds in front of me. He (I think it was a male bird) was soon joined by a second Grebe, which appeared from the direction of the island.

The birds came together, chest to chest, necks stretched up, hoods expanded, the fine filaments of each bird's crest raised in two fan-like shapes. Now commenced a vigorous, alternate head-shaking, which terminated in a series of graceful posturings, in which each bird pretended to pluck a feather from its lower-back and offer it to its mate. In this latter phase of the display the form of their sinuous necks was beautiful to watch. Gradually they made an end of the performance and separated, each going its own way.

CHARLES TUNNICLIFFE

GREBE DISPLAY – SECOND POSITION

DABCHICK PREPARING TO LEAVE THE NEST

The re-appearance of the Dabchick was greeted by a little rippling call from the sitting bird, which had now lowered its neck and raised a ridge of feathers along its nape. With seeming reluctance it raised itself on legs placed far back on turtle-shaped body, and pulled at the nest material. I saw one egg only, and this the bird did not cover completely before it shuffled off the nest and into the water. Its mate at once climbed up the opposite side of the nest, re-arranged the nest-material, and settled on the white elongated-oval egg.

CHARLES TUNNICLIFFE

DUCK AND RIVAL SUITORS

CANADAS ABOUT TO ALIGHT

A thin crescent moon showed itself in the south-west as the light began to fail, and I was about to turn away from watching a small flock of Canada Geese when two of them, which were grazing on the pasture, began to honk excitedly and, the larger of the pair chasing the other, rose into the air, still loudly clamouring. Passing over my head at a height of not more than thirty feet, they made a complete circuit of the pasture, just clearing the tops of some of the oaks and flying between others. They swept round, setting their wings for the glide down; then, with tail widely expanded, feet out, landed on the water with a curve of spray on each side of them. More excited honking followed, with the gander jerkily bowing to the goose, his rigid neck swaying up and down as he swam with her to the bank. A minute afterwards they repeated the whole performance.

CHARLES TUNNICLIFFE

OULTON MERE

*A*pril came in with a smile. The morning was lovely with dreamy sunlight and balmy air. One almost expected to hear the sound of mowing machines and the humming of bees in the trees. But the grass was still sere and lifeless, and the lime-tree buds were yet fast closed.

Unable to resist, I put down my tools at noon, and the early afternoon found W. and I following the winding path through the trees of Oulton woods to the sound of drumming Woodpeckers. There the mere was a place of soft reflections: herds of deer were grazing on both banks, and their hoof-prints were everywhere on the soft ground.

CHARLES TUNNICLIFFE

DABCHICK

BUDWORTH POOL

*S*lipping down to Budworth Pool we watched the storm rumble away westwards; the rain ceased, and behold, our first Swallow of the year came skimming over the water. We took our hats off to it. It did not tarry with us long, but was away over the pastures and we soon lost sight of it.

Presently, four Sand-martins came to the pool and hawked after the low-flying insects, and, as the afternoon drew on, their company was increased to a dozen. Below them a Grebe was fishing, and, to our amusement, came up with a large roach in almost exactly the same place as did the Grebe on our last visit to Budworth Pool, and had the same great difficulty in swallowing the fish. We wondered if he made a habit of entertaining all visitors in this manner.

CHARLES TUNNICLIFFE

BATHING PARTY

RADNOR MERE FROM THE WOODS

Clamour of geese greeted us this morning even before we were in sight of the mere, and when we came on to the bank we saw seven noisy and excited Canadas posing and posturing on the water. They were honking with a deep, clanging note, and as their excitement increased the calling grew higher in pitch and frequency. Suddenly, when their clamour seemed to have reached its climax, they all took wing, running over the water, necks outstretched and wing-tips whipping the surface until they rose clear. They swept round the mere and returned in grand style, wings set, and feet stretched out to plough the water as they alighted. Again, after much honking, two, which I think were ganders, took wing and flew swiftly round, one following closely on the tail of the other. This looked like a chase, and when they landed the pursuer swam to a smaller goose, his necked outstretched along the rippled water, seeming to ask loudly for her approval of his chase of the rival gander.

CHARLES TUNNICLIFFE

THE ISLAND IN THE UPPER POOL

*T*he chestnut branches which overhang the water-side all had their finials and crockets of down-pointing young leaves, beautiful in their virile shapes and vivid colour against the sparkling mere, which, in the sun's track, reflected myriads of dazzling points.

The strong breeze which blew down the mere brought with it the sound of geese, and as I walked clear of the trees I saw seven Canadas swimming near the opposite bank and, at the same time, heard more goose clamour coming from beyond the wood at my back.

CHARLES TUNNICLIFFE

YOUNG CORMORANT AND AN EEL

CANADA ON NEST

Continuing along the barely defined mere-side path through the hummocks of dead rush, I came to the neck of land which divides the Mere from the Upper Pool. Nothing stirred on the pool except one, solitary, Canada gander which cruised about restlessly. As I drew nearer he became most uneasy and vented a high-pitched, warning, call. I began to look for his mate and soon I espied her, sitting on a nest at the foot of the gnarled trunk of a willow growing on the little island in the pool. She had her back towards me and her dull brown plumage harmonized perfectly with its surroundings, looking very like a fallen log of wood. Her black neck, laid flat along the edge of the nest, was turned towards me, and her black, beady eye regarded me intently.

CHARLES TUNNICLIFFE

CANADAS THROUGH THE LILIES

THE DAB CHICK'S NEST

This morning I found the car with a punctured back tyre. I pumped it up and left it at a garage for repair and while the work was being done, walked up to the pool in South Park, not expecting to see anything but the usual motley crowd of Ducks, the two Swans and a few Moorhens.

But it is an ill wind that blows no one good, for that puncture resulted in the discovery of two Dabchick on the pool.

The first indication of their presence was a high, whinnying call which came from the willows at the lower corner of the water. Soon I was able to pick out, among the willow tangle, the sunlit chestnut cheeks and fluffy, buff sterns of the two Dabchick. . . .

Threading their way through the mazes of the low-growing willows the Dabchicks swam to a heap of black, rotted vegetation, and one bird mounted this heap and sat on it. A wetter, more uninviting place to sit was difficult to imagine. When the swimming bird dived and came up carrying more rotting vegetation which it placed on the heap I had to believe that this was a nest. After several dives, each of which produced a black and dripping addition, the working Dabchick mounted the nest and sat beside its mate which, owing to my long scrutiny through the glasses, had dropped head and neck onto the nest.

The sun shone on chestnut heads and glossy, lead-grey backs and picked out with startling contrast the pale yellow-green skin at the angle of the mouth.

While one bird worked, busily re-arranging the nest-stuff, the other preened its wings, revealing the small, delicately curved flights. They puffed out the downy feathers of backs and rumps, sure sign that they were at ease and untroubled. (A Dabchick that is alarmed or uneasy is a tight, slim little bird).

CHARLES TUNNICLIFFE

THE BLASÉ COOT

*W*hen I pulled up under the trees at the "car-park" corner of the mere, that very blasé Coot was sitting on its nest in the reed-bed and did not trouble even to raise its head when I got out of the car. Nor was it alarmed by a violent splashing which was shaking the reed-stems near the nest.

I could not at first see what was making the disturbance, but could trace the movement of something travelling through the reed-bed as the stalks suddenly shook and then were still again.

More splashings happened simultaneously from several places in the reeds and I was still puzzled until, in one of the turmoils, two grey-green, humped backs broke the surface. Then I saw that they were bream for, as one flopped over, it showed a glimpse of pale-gold undersides and a depth of body and a thinness of back which could belong to no other fish.

It was evidently spawning time, as that is the only purpose for which the bream enter such shallow water. I only wish that those disgruntled fishermen who spend their days watching their ever-still, and highly-coloured floats and growling that they have "never 'ad a bite this season" could have seen the sight. They would, at least, have been filled with hope.

CHARLES TUNNICLIFFE

CROAKING CUCKOOS BY LOCH GLENDHU

In the birch trees growing from the rocks above our heads, three Cuckoos alighted, making the most devilish and witch-like croaks as they rocked and turned in the slender branches. Two flew off to another tree while the one that was left, a male bird, croaked and gurgled spasmodically as he swivelled on the branch and swung his tail from side to side. The two and two arrangement of his toes was very easily seen from below.

The Cuckoos continued to dash from one tree to another until their capers were interrupted by the sudden arrival of a Tit-lark which furiously attacked and chased one of them. The two remaining Cuckoos perched and croaked, now with raised tail half-spread and wing-tips dropped, now swinging and swivelling, quite oblivious of our presence beneath them. Presently they made off up the gorse-golden hillside, still uttering their weird, un-birdlike noises.

CHARLES TUNNICLIFFE

NORTH RODE POOL

Leaving Bosley we went through the quiet countryside to North Rode Pool. Here a great quietness prevailed and the tip, tip of leaves falling through the branches only intensified the stillness. Even the noise of the water running into the outlet shaft, usually so loud and persistent, was quietened to the merest murmur and, standing as we were with a huge beech intervening, could scarcely be heard.

The sloping park land with its clumps of tall trees and the white Manor House inverted themselves in the glassy surface, and the splashes of orange-vermilion horse-chestnut foliage were just as vivid in their mirrored image as on the tree itself.

We returned along the rough-surfaced lane, our every stride accompanied by the swishing sound of crisp, dead leaves and the crackle and crunch of beech nuts under our feet. We felt that we had had our fill of beauty for one day.

CHARLES TUNNICLIFFE

HERON GLIDING DOWN

ROOKS AND JACKDAWS MOBBING A HERON

From Autumn into Winter. The mere-side bushes had shed their leaves, and the willows were spangled with the last yellow remnants of theirs.

From the direction of the school came a sudden loud clamour of Rooks and Jackdaws, and over the trees appeared a black mob swirling about the grey shape of a loudly protesting Heron, which tipped and side-slipped to avoid the continuous attacks of his stooping tormentors. They harried him until he came to rest on a mere-side alder, on a branch half way down the tree. Above him perched the Rooks and Jackdaws, awaiting his next move.

After five minutes of unmolested rest among the catkin-covered branches the big grey bird launched himself from the tree, and was at once surrounded by the rowdy mob again. The swooping, stooping, swirling crowd of black devils chased the Heron down the mere, and did not leave him until he gained the refuge of the tall trees of Boathouse Wood.

CHARLES TUNNICLIFFE

RELEASING THE BIRD

SHIRE AND GROOM

ACKNOWLEDGEMENTS

LINCOLN CURLY-COATED SOW

The publisher acknowledges with gratitude the assistance and co-operation of the Estate of the late C. F. Tunnicliffe, the publishers of the various books from which illustrations and text have been taken, and other bodies who have loaned pictures for reproduction in this book. In particular thanks are due to Commander W. Braddock, Arthur Campey and Philip Craghill who, along with the other members of the Tunnicliffe family, have offered hospitality and practical help, including the loan of original artwork. Others whose help has been invaluable in various ways include Chris Perfect, Ian Stoner, Graham Sadd, David Burnett, Roger Houghton, Alison Thomas, Mr. Glyn Jones and the Anglesey Borough Council; Mr. Nicholas Hammond and the R.S.P.B.; Mr. Francis Farmer and Christie Manson and Wood Ltd; Miss Mary Axon and the National Museum of Wales. We acknowledge the kindness of Collier Macmillan Ltd, William Collins Ltd, Faber and Faber Ltd, William Heinemann Ltd, The Hamlyn Publishing Group Ltd, Hodder and Stoughton Ltd, Messrs. Lutterworth Press, Methuen, London Ltd and Victor Gollancz Ltd in giving us permission to use extracts from their books, full details of which are given in the bibliography. Illustrations and text reproduced from the "Ladybird" books, *What to Look for in Spring*, *What to Look for in Summer*, *What to Look for in Autumn* and *What to Look for in Winter* are reproduced with the permission of the publishers, Ladybird Books Ltd, Loughborough, Leicestershire, England. Illustrations from *Tarka the Otter*, *The Lone Swallows and Other Tales* and *The Old Stag* by Henry Williamson, *Beasts Royal* by Patrick Russ and *Tales from Ebony* by Harcourt Williams, are reproduced by permission of The Bodley Head.

We are most grateful to Mrs. Dorothy Downes, Charles Tunnicliffe's sister, for the interest she has taken in this project and for her practical assistance. Above all, thanks are due to Ian Niall for his advice and encouragement, so freely given, and to his wife Sheila, for her hospitality. It was as a result of his kind letter of congratulation following the republication of *Going Fishing*, and the subsequent days of discussion on the riverside (and in the country pubs) that this book was conceived.

BIBLIOGRAPHY

HEDGE-SPARROW FEEDING YOUNG CUCKOO

A Book of Birds by Mary Priestley. Victor Gollancz, 1937.

Adventuring with Nomad by Norman Ellison. University of London Press, 1950.

A Fowler's World by Ian Niall. Heinemann, 1968.

A Galloway Childhood by Ian Niall. Heinemann, 1967.

Ambush of Young Days by Alison Uttley. Faber and Faber, 1951.

Beasts Royal by Richard Patrick Russ. Putnam, 1934.

Bird Portraiture. The Studio, 1945.

Both Sides of the Road by Sidney Rogerson and Charles Tunnicliffe. Collins, 1949.

Dawn, Dusk and Deer by Arthur Cadman. Country Life, 1966.

Exploring England by Charles S. Bayne. William Collins, 1944.

Going Fishing by Negley Farson. Country Life, 1942.

Green Tide by Richard Church. Country Life, 1945.

In the Heart of the Country by H. E. Bates. Country Life, 1942.

Mereside Chronicle. Country Life, 1948.

My Country Book. The Studio, 1942.

Northwards with Nomad by Norman Ellison. University of London Press, 1951.

O More Than Happy Countryman by H. E. Bates. Country Life, 1943.

Our Bird Book by Sidney Rogerson and Charles Tunnicliffe. Collins, 1947.

Out of Doors with Nomad by Norman Ellison. University of London Press, 1947.

Over the Hills with Nomad by Norman Ellison. University of London Press, 1948.

Plowmen's Clocks by Alison Uttley. Faber and Faber, 1952.

Rivermouth by Brian Vesey-Fitzgerald. Eyre and Spottiswoode, 1949.

Roving with Nomad by Norman Ellison. University of London Press, 1949.

R.S.P.B. Book of Garden Birds by Linda Bennett. Hamlyn, 1978.

Salar the Salmon by Henry Williamson. Faber and Faber, 1935. First illustrated edition, October 1936.

Shorelands Summer Diary. Collins, 1952.

Tales from Ebony by Harcourt Williams. Putnam, 1934.

Tarka the Otter by Henry Williamson. Putnam, 1932.

The Country Child by Alison Uttley. Faber and Faber, 1945.

The Farm on the Hill by Alison Uttley. Faber and Faber, 1949.

The Leaves Return by E. L. Grant Watson. Country Life, 1947.

The Lone Swallows by Henry Williamson. Putnam, 1933.

The Long Flight by Terence Horsley. Country Life, 1947.

The Old Stag by Henry Williamson. Putnam, 1933.

The Way of a Countryman by Ian Niall. Country Life, 1965.

Walking with Fancy by E. L. Grant Watson. Country Life, 1943.

Wild Life in a Southern County by Richard Jefferies. Lutterworth Press, 1949.

What to Look for in Autumn by E. L. Grant Watson. Wills and Hepworth, 1960. (A "Ladybird" Book, Series 536).

What to Look for in Spring by E. L. Grant Watson. Wills and Hepworth, 1961. (A "Ladybird" Book, Series 536).

What to Look for in Summer by E. L. Grant Watson. Wills and Hepworth, 1960 (A "Ladybird" Book, Series 536).

What to Look for in Winter by E. L. Grant Watson. Wills and Hepworth, 1959. (A "Ladybird" Book, Series 536).

LIST OF ILLUSTRATIONS

INTERESTED SPECTATOR

LIST OF ILLUSTRATIONS

STARTLED PHEASANT

LIST OF ILLUSTRATIONS

WOODPIGEON

LIST OF ILLUSTRATIONS

FINIS